What people are saying about

Story C

Carol Day is an extraordinary, inn…   …u girted practitioner, teacher and Author. She brings in the power of love, compassion and creativity to all of her work. In *Story Compass*, she takes us deep into the unseen worlds and provides a rich and meaningful experience for all.

Sandra Ingerman, MA, world renowned shamanic teacher and Author of 12 books including *Walking in Light* and *The Book of Ceremony*

Carol Day has written an imaginative book that takes the reader with her, as Co-Navigator, across the seas of the stories and Myths that make up our lives. It's a voyage of self-discovery and will support the reader to know themselves better as step-by-step, Carol supports us to know where we are, where we come from, and where we are going. Enjoy the journey.

Ya'Acov Darling Khan, Shaman, Best-Selling Author of *Jaguar in the Body, Butterfly in the Heart* and *Shaman - Invoking Power, presence and Purpose at The Core of Who You Are* and Co-Founder of Movement Medicine

What a delight this is! I felt a beautiful wave of excitement creeping up from my toes into my belly as I started to dive in as if I was a child going through the wardrobe into Narnia. The richness of the subject and creative way of guiding the reader through the visionary *Story Compass* practice creates an inspirational and fluid space for the reader to take control and begin to conjure our own magic. This book feels like a timely reminder and a gentle nudge that we are the creators of our own stories and we hold the power to steer our course through the theatre of life. Carol

Day is a creative visionary and it's hard not to follow this book without feeling the same. This work is more than a guide through the realm of story, it reunites us with the supportive guidance of nature and empowers and inspires hope.

Fay Johnstone, Author of *Plants that Speak Souls that Sing: Transform your Life with the Spirit of Plants* and *Plant Spirit Reiki: Energy Healing with the Elements of Nature*

Getting to know and honouring all our parts is what makes life exciting and opens us up to our creativity. Some of us are lucky to discover a way to do this on our own. However, occasionally a gem arrives on our doorstep. *Story Compass* is such a safe, strong companion supporting us to find the new lenses to free us from an old story by creating our own new story. A beautifully written book that takes us into the dreaming with ease, guiding us with drumming, writing, ritual, myth and more to bring our dreaming into everyday life to live with new vigour. Thank you, Carol, this book is a tour de force and much needed for those who love the journey inwards.

Sarena Wolfaard, process oriented psychotherapist, movement teacher and publisher

I feel like this should be called the story of everything! Because it literally reveals stories everywhere and in everything - narratives playing out in your life, in nature and in the wider world. It causes you to question your everything and gives you the tools to find the answers. It's an experiential book - it's incredibly playful and encourages you to let go (have a dress up box and crayons at the ready) and Carol has a way of making your life feel fun and magical, but at the same time the practices in this book are deep. It's got me hooked on archetype and myth and has helped me understand why I love storytelling and became a filmmaker. But this book is about more than just creating stories – it's about deep listening. It teaches you that you can be the author and the reader of your world, both of which are useful tools to navigate your life with consciousness and clarity, and how the two are constantly playing out in your life at any given moment.

Janine Finlay, Producer/Director Fin Films Ltd

In her new book Carol Day takes the role of Narrator so you get to be a Navigator! You can follow the Pole Star or be a Pole (Dancing) Star! You are encouraged to visit the Place of Ancestral Stories and add your own stories to the hoard. By reading this book you enter the magical mystery zone where nothing is impossible and everything exists in an infinity of manifestations. Be a star - follow the lode star - find your inner stars! Carol's work never fails to enchant me because she weaves her visionary web and invites others to embark on journeys, soul voyages, quests. This is the Narrator in the role of Navigator at her very best! Gift yourself a powerful tool: a *Story Compass*!

Imelda Almqvist, international teacher and Author of three books including *Sacred Art: A Hollow Bone for Spirit* and *Medicine of the Imagination: Dwelling in Possibility (An Impassioned Plea for Fearless Imagination)*

As you carry this book with you, you carry a portable workshop for healing through presence, imagination, curiosity, and truth. We are all navigating the seas of our lives. Carol's work offers a compass and a rudder to take us to the best possible versions of ourselves. This is a book that can be read and reread as one uses the Story process to shed light on the meaning of his or her circumstances, life lessons, aspirations, intentions, and relationships. She has an artist's delightful and creative way of weaving healing through magic and whimsy, truth and honesty, even our biggest shadows and doubts. The participant accesses, through the neutrality of observation and presence, their greatest potential. This book is a great resource for living an authentic life. Discover your own personal Myth and magic through the pages of this enchanting read.

Janet Gale, Author of *The Rush Hour Shaman*

Twenty-five years ago, when I was working as a teacher with, among other things, duties as a pastoral Counsellor, I combined my love of literature with my skills as a Counsellor and turned my sessions into opportunities whereby my clients could take a healing journey into the realm of the imagination, memory, and story. Of course, today, one can find many examples of the use of storytelling in psychotherapy — from the archetypal psychology of C.G. Jung to narrative therapy pioneered by Michael White and David Epston, and to Ken Land's Storytelling Therapy ™. Carol Day's *Story Compass* takes this therapeutic work out of the closed therapist's office and into the hands of the reader. This is not an academic text-book but an exciting invitation to take a journey aboard the "Good Ship Story" with Carol and a host of archetypal entities as your companions. Of course, you are the captain; after all, this is your story.

Carol invites you to set sail on a 'Mythological sea' (your life) on a voyage that "leads us through the veils and beyond the edges of death". No need to fear for this is a metaphorical journey that, like poetry, calls for the suspension of disbelief. You are embarking on an interactive journey into your Imagination. The book is more a navigator's chart of old where not everywhere is clearly marked. Carol inspires you to use your creativity to find your way using art, visualisation, music, movement, and story to guide you. This aptly named book is your *'story compass'* that will guide you on your own personal "vision quest" through the four cardinal directions: North (Author), East (Lifeline), South (Ancestors), and West (Myth). Each section encourages you to reflect on your stories and experiences in a metaphorical and archetypal context. Carol provides the Mythical structure and archetypal references such as the anchor, the sea, the ship, the map, and others. She also offers a range of exercises, some requiring journaling and others involving singing, drumming, movement, visualisation, artwork, and meditation. As she says, you can do as much as you need to and you can dip into the book as feels right for you; or, you can begin at the beginning and spend six months or more making the journey.

This idea of the 'story journey' bears a parallel with other creative works such as Julia Cameron's *The Artist's Way* or Natalie Goldberg's *Writing Down the Bones*. Like Cameron and Goldberg, Day's work is based on years of working with writers, storytellers, and others, exploring the creative imagination through Myth and archetypes. I highly recommend Carol Day's *Story Compass* as your guide, helping you to chart a course to the Mythical realms of story and the unbounded horizon of your imagination.

Michael Williams, Storyteller, Story Coach, Writer

Carol's lyrical writing takes you step by step on the journey through story. Clearly laid out, easy to follow with weekly tasks to guide and help you become a Story worker. Stories are woven through out and the whole book is imbued with enthusiasm and joy.

My experience with Carol's earlier work, The Story Apprentice, led to deepening of my relationship with story as a Storyteller and a person. *Story Compass* will continue that path even further in an easily accessible format for anyone who wishes to take the journey. Set sail aboard the Good Ship Story for Carol is an inspiring and expert navigator.

Lindsey Gibb, Storyteller and Co-Author of *Perthshire Tales*

Our lives are a tapestry of tales. Ancestral threads alongside years of weaving on the loom of life, creates our own unique book. Within the folds of our stories, we will find both the victim and the hero. What Carol invites each of us to do is to untangle the knots to celebrate the hero. *Story Compass* is an exceptional guide, a gem of a map, and like anything worth its salt, it requires active participation for the shifts to occur. Enjoy the ride and be willing to invest in your journey. In so doing, the guides, the Pole Star and this treasure map will serve your ship well as you sail into the adventures awaiting you on the high seas.

Andrew Steed, Best Selling Author, including *Powering Up Our Life Stories*

This fascinating work explores the wider realms of narrative identity. *Story Compass* is the exposition of the Author's approach in writing this book. It is both the methodology and the book itself. Her narrative is eclectic, encompassing the skills of the Story Practitioner, artist, teacher, Counsellor, and many more, calling on nature, Mythological landscapes, and archetypes. It is a manual on how to write your own book, your inner book, your life story. It is also a self-help manual, as well as an account of the Author's journey to complete her own inner story.

Julia McLeod, Author of *Personal and Professional Development for Counsellors, Psychotherapists and Mental Health Practitioners* and *Counselling Skills: A Practical Guide for Counsellors and Helping Professionals*

We all live by stories whether that be the story we tell ourselves and wrote for ourselves or whether that be stores written by others that we live by. Carol allows you to open your heart to your story to see who has influenced it and how changing it can be a powerful healing journey not only for yourself but also for those who have gone before you and those who come after you. The connection and trust with and of nature throughout is deeply magical and profound.

Lyn Hill, Founder of *Sacred Awakenings*

This book is an innovative self-help manual designed especially for would-be creative writers. The narrator, who is in fact the Author reflecting on what has helped her, sees the creative process as a journey through her own life experiences, those of ancestors and of Mythological characters, which will progressively unlock the creative instinct. Along the way she recommends exercises and activities which will assist in this process. A beautiful and inspiring story!

Jan Keane, Author of *National Identity an Education in Early Twentieth Century Australia*

This is a delightful and distinctive offering in the concept of Story work and guided journeying. Carol Day offers a meaningful and spiritual way of exploring ourselves through the nature of story... incorporating nature, creativity and harnessing the authentic self within us.

Allie Scott, Accredited Counsellor, Mental Health Practitioner and Trainer

I work with people with profound and multiple learning disabilities. The course that accompanies this book takes multi-sensory stories to a new level. Stories are important in our lives and the stories of people with profound and multiple learning disabilities are often not heard, yet these people are our biggest educators. This book opens up a whole new way of being for this group.

Maureen Phillip, Founder of *Spirit of Stories*, PAMIS

This journey with story was phenomenal... safely held and navigated, I explored new territories and vast seas and embarked home, crowned with a deeper understanding of the mystery and magic that abounds me.

Sarah Milne, Priestess of the Wilds, Visionary artist, Story Practitioner and Perpetual Dreamer

Carol Day is an authentic treasure trove of wisdom and accomplishment. She can lead you through Story work and help heal the scary places of your autobiography with ease and grace. Invaluable!

Francesca Aniballi, Teacher, Expressive Arts Therapist and Facilitator, Creative Coach and Writer

Story Compass

An unprecedented journey of discovery
with myth and life

Story Compass

An unprecedented journey of discovery
with myth and life

Carol Day

**MOON
BOOKS**

Winchester, UK
Washington, USA

JOHN HUNT PUBLISHING

First published by Moon Books, 2022
Moon Books is an imprint of John Hunt Publishing Ltd., No. 3 East Street, Alresford
Hampshire SO24 9EE, UK
office@jhpbooks.net
www.johnhuntpublishing.com
www.moon-books.net

For distributor details and how to order please visit the 'Ordering' section on our website.

Text copyright: Carol Day 2021

ISBN: 978 1 78904 850 6
978 1 78904 851 3 (ebook)
Library of Congress Control Number: 2021934883

A CIP catalogue record for this book is available from the British Library.

Design: Stuart Davies

UK: Printed and bound by CPI Group (UK) Ltd, Croydon, CR0 4YY
Printed in North America by CPI GPS partners

We operate a distinctive and ethical publishing philosophy in
all areas of our business, from our global network of authors to
production and worldwide distribution.

Contents

Other books by Carol Day

Wheel 2017 ISBN 978-1-78808-432-1 and 978-1-78808-250-1

Drum 2018 ISBN 978-1-78808-323-2 and 978-1-78808-324-9

For the Mythical Ones

"It is probable that the next Buddha will not take the form of an individual. The next Buddha may take the form of a community, a community practicing understanding and loving kindness, a community practicing mindful living, applying wisdom to life with each other. This may be the most important thing we can do for the survival of the earth."

Thich Nhat Hanh

Acknowledgements

Firstly, I acknowledge the five ship mates who set sail on this journey with me in its test form: Maureen Phillip, Francesca Aniballi, Lyn Hill, Sarah Milne and Daniela Meier – thank you! You kept me afloat, filled me with awe and jollied me along.

To Dave, you gave me the sturdiest of shores to return to when I went out so far into the other worlds. Thank you.

To my mother Ann, you have always brought me up to shine my light. I don't know where you come from, but it's a place from a magical future, for sure.

To all the people who have ever come to work and play with these ideas that come, thank you for believing in something. In the joy of my work with each of you, I forget that the world out there is not always so enlightened and full of hope.

To David Greig, thank you for thinking writing the foreword for this book was a good idea and for writing one so brilliantly. It enhances everything herein and is an inspiring article in itself.

To Sarah Roberts, Anna Williamson, Anna Heinrich and all of my old Art college friends of the 1980s, thank you for being the bedrock of fun and creativity that is the soil my current self constantly grows from. We were lucky to have those beginnings into adulthood. To Art colleges everywhere, keep putting the creative spirit first; its narrative weaves a magic that keeps the world alive.

To my son Arin Beaver and daughter Tsen Day-Beaver for the illumination of your architect and actor souls.

To everyone who supported my initiatory growth through shamanic, counselling and artistic education routes, I am forever grateful for your helping me to learn how to better hold this cosmic, sometimes imploding, human.

To my ancestors who planted the seeds for my quest, thank you for making sure that my life was never dull and for always putting in front of me what I need next. The older I get, the more I feel you. I look forward to the great party when one day I come to join you again.

To the archetypes of the lands of Myth and whatever great blessing I got to be able to see, hear and communicate with you, you are my raison d'être. May you always find a way to wake me up!

To my life, this planet and oh my what a story! You are the most incredible creation and I will never stop trying to understand how you work and how to be effective inside you.

Which leads me to my dad, my fellow engineer. Perhaps we are the only ones who will ever realise just how similar we are. I miss you.

And finally, to Moon Books for taking the step to pick up this book and run with it, thank you for helping to take these ideas out there and for your faith and support.

Foreword

The human encounter with story has always been transcendental. Which is to say, that the realm of story, as we experience it, is a world beyond this world. It's a world the size of this world, bigger even. It's a world parallel to us, or above us, or in our collective heads, or in our dreams. Wherever it is located, the realm of story it is most definitely somewhere you can't enter physically, with your own body. To access the realm of story, you need to lose yourself.

Entering the realm of story is child's play. Which means it's easy if you're a child, but very difficult if you're an adult. Watch a child when they play... manipulating objects, creating worlds, inventing characters, dialogue pouring out of them...but, the moment we adults draw attention to them; by praising them, or documenting the play, or putting a photo of them on Facebook – the magic departs. We have brought self and the world into the world of story and the entryway has closed up again. Adults find it hard to lose ourselves as we have so much self to lose, and we are all so armoured and laden with baggage!

In fact, in my experience as a playwright, playing is the single hardest task in the creation of a play. Once I have successfully found my way 'in' to the world of story it feels easy, even pleasurable, to wander round and explore. In that world, what I need comes to me just as I need it and all I have to do is write it all down as it happens. But oh, getting there is so hard!

That is why it helps to have a guide and Carol Day is a brilliant guide: imaginative, patient, experienced, careful, light and witty. Carol has worked with me on two different occasions, using many of the methods outlined in this book. In each case her patient work and delightful interventions helped me to take off my everyday suit of armour and enter a mindspace of light and play... in other words, she helped me

3

access the realm of story.

In this book Carol lays out a map, and offers some simple, practical advice to help you find your own way into the realm of story, and she gives you some tools to help you explore once you're there.

Carol's work is more than just writing exercises. It's a daily practice which opens you up and changes you. Her metaphors come from adventure, navigation and exploration and these are very appropriate for stepping into another world. Carol, and the fascinating spirits she conjures, are the perfect guides to let you into this world, to make you feel comfortable, and then to let you play.

Of course, you don't have to be a playwright or a novelist to explore story, the world is open to everyone. Making up stories is about far more than the simple provision of entertainment. Story is the very engineering, the plumbing of our inner lives. Story is how we access emotion and self-understanding. By finding and telling stories, we work out who we are and, crucially, we give ourselves the chance to re-arrange the pipes through which our emotions flow.

I remember, in 2019, watching a revival of my first proper play 'Europe' at the Donmar Warehouse Theatre in London. I was watching it nearly twenty five years after I wrote it. What stunned me, as I sat in the audience, was how nakedly I had revealed my younger self. At the time of writing, I had had no idea how much of my internal story I was working out on stage. I genuinely thought I was writing a Brechtian play about the collapse of communism. In fact, it turns out, I was writing a story about a young man wrestling with the question of whether to stay or to leave: a job, a country, a relationship, a dream… I thought it was just a story I'd made up. I should have known. Nothing in the realm of story is 'just made up.' Looking back, I can see that writing that play was my own way of exploring a question I deeply needed to answer for myself.

Story is fundamental to our experience of being human because the realm of story is where grown-ups play. You may be reading this book because you wish to write a play, or a novel or a film, and this book will definitely help you do that. But whether you want to create an object with your stories and share them with the world, or whether you just want to whisper your stories to yourself. I would still recommend this book because, simply, if you follow its practice, you will re-discover a doorway into a place of play, and that's a gift beyond price.

David Greig, Playwright 25th January 2021

Preface

The material for this book came through joyfully and urgently right on cue, as the covid-19 story hit the UK. I spent six months producing the material, working alongside five international storytellers who by good fortune came along to join the journey. Together, we spent six months at sea. Being on the Good Ship Story has been one of the deepest, strangest (lockdown!) and highly spirited periods of my life. I come out of writing the last words of this tale, instantaneously mailing it through the ether to a publisher. I am trusting that the archives of the Mythological landscape the journey of this book explores and the power of the archetypes who have overseen the writing of it will somehow find a way to bring it to you and to many more who are destined to bring the practice of 'story understanding' back into the world.

You see there aren't really that many people who understand story. I meet folk who tell stories really well. I know many teachers who brilliantly encourage creative story making for others. I am a friend with a great number of people who counsel with adeptness and skill, scouring through the story fields of clients to enable each one to find a clear space for themselves. I am a peer with artists who penetrate the art story field with pristine precision and effectiveness. But I honestly haven't come across many people who do all of these things together and have the multiplicity of lenses on the 'what story is, what it does and how we interact with it' that results in the story understanding that this body of work affords a resurrection and new direction for.

As I write, the wind has picked up and is howling around the house. The last week of writing has brought floods that moved me out of my practice home and the most incredible thunder and lightning storms I have seen since I was trapped in the air on the way back from Santa Fe on level with the lightning beings. On that occasion, I had spent the previous evening merging with Athena at a Shamanic Theatre event. Athena was the only Goddess or God of the Parthenon who was permitted to carry the lightning bolt other than Zeus. Again, I felt her presence, watching the sky forked by lightning beings I had sat on a level with in years gone by. Perhaps they reawakened a part of me as this last week has included dreams of water, rivers, seas and mountains speaking to me like never before and the euphoria of serendipity I haven't felt for a long time. I feel that this piece of work is the birthing of a clear realm.

I owe the credit of the experience of being able to bring this material through, to nature and story. Firstly, to nature, whom I have been steadfastly returning to and calling myself back into since I experienced entry to the wider story realms three decades ago. On many occasions I have heard the mountains speaking and felt the plants and weather calling. I have known there had to be a way to return to nature again as a human and to be able to experience the world forever in this open, communicating way. I also knew that it was the Fairy stories and Myths I had hidden for hours in libraries as a child to read that had the keys to unlock this relationship for us all again. And as you will find in this book - they do!

I want to thank Marcie, whose passion with the story of the Titanic and the watching of the film together the night before I was due to start writing this material gave me the inspiration for the Good Ship Story. Here is a ship that doesn't sink and yet whose voyage does lead us through the veils and beyond the formless edge of death.

My books are interactive. I am a bit of a Roland Barthes 'Death of the Author' appreciation society. I have been writing material that is what I call 'visionary questing' for some time. I love to dream, to creatively weave and to open up new possibilities, but realise that it is what we do and the rituals we bring into this life that will build a new way. Beyond the visioning, we have to get up and make action that can create change. So, this book, if you want to experience it to the full, can be a six-month long exploration of your everyday life. It is however *your* book and it is written for you and your inner knowing that has led you to choose it, so please just trust your own way and timings. You might dip into bits at different times and you may want to come into port regularly on different lands. Whatever you need to do will be your story.

I just hope this book can help free story, help nature, humans and Myth to weave their way harmoniously together again and ultimately help you to be more of you!

Bon voyage!

Carol Day

Arcadia, Scotland

Introduction

A Manual

Welcome to *Story Compass* and welcome aboard the Good Ship Story! This good ship will sail all who work and play with story.

So, firstly, let's enter the space of imagination. Imagine that it is night. Feel yourself landing on this vessel and notice the sound of the lap of the water on the ship's sides. Can you lean over the side to see the water in the moonlit depths below? See how black it is and how the surface glints whilst rippling. Come across the deck, now. Here, to the Captain's spot. I invite you to take your rightful place on this ship and to take in your hands the trusty ship's wheel. Here it is, with its wooden circle and the cross pointers to the four directions. Hold it tight. This is your ship and your Story Practice. Feel a cap that would befit a captain take its place on your head. Take ownership right now. You are the captain of your own Story Practice. What you read here is a rustic manual that will help you to remember what you already know about this ancient craft. It is written in your bones. It is also written in the stars.

With this known, look above you to search with your eyes the deep night skies. Can you see the Pole Star up there that all sailors follow to find their bearings? It is sometimes known as the North Star. You can set your sights on the Pole Star and know that with the support of the Pole Star's presence navigation can begin!

Here you are holding the philosophy of the 4Directions Story model in your hands and in your gaze. By being at the ship's wheel with the Pole Star as a guide and the rudder at hand you will be able to steer your way to your destination.

In *Story Compass*, the sea is your life and the ship is your body. The wheel and the North Star are the tools for the practice.

The destination is whatever you set your course for and is the intention you bring to this book now! Take some moments to contemplate this. Perhaps take some notes.

- How is your body (the ship) feeling about this journey (across the sea)?
- How is your body (the ship) relating to your life (the sea)?
- Where even is the Pole Star?
- What is the Pole Star to you?
- What is the wheel that you can hold in your hands that steers through North, South, East and West?
- How do you feel these four directions in your body (the ship)?
- Where is the rudder?
- What is your destination?
- What are you putting out for in picking up this book?

Ethos

Here is the ship's manual bit about the ethos of this work: You are on a journey to understand the role of a Story worker. The role you will be encouraged to hold as a Story worker is clear. It is simply that by stepping onto a journey that allows even more understanding of the way of story, each of us is able to be more present and effective for others in bringing restorative power to the stories each of us tell or live in our lives.

Sailing on the Good Ship Story is an imagined experience that can support you to investigate and understand story's way. Sometimes I imagine the botanists who sailed the seas in Victorian expeditions to bring back rare species of plants and trees to study them. Well, here is an expedition for us now, except that the study is of the expedition itself and the findings are about what can be useful to allow a Story Practice to flow from it.

Expedition Course

The expedition is organised to help each of us to follow the way of story as it operates through four principle realms of our lives. The directions the ship's wheel refers to taking you to explore hold these realms: North, South, East and West. By setting the course to each in turn, in the end you will come back to where you began, seeing life and its story afresh.

As T.S. Elliot writes,

We shall not cease from exploration
And the end of all our exploring
Will be to arrive where we started
And know the place for the first time.

Each of these directions will lead you to four different realms. These realms will relate to the experiences and lenses that are included in our story making lives.

The ship will take you first in a Northerly direction into the realm of you and your body - the lens of the Author. Then you will head East into the realm of the lifeline and the lens and experience of your lived life. Naturally, South will come next and you will enter the place of the ancestral lens and lives lived. Finally, West will call you and you will visit the realm of the archetypes, the forces of creation and the place of Myth, imagination and nature.

Through exploring and seeing better the way that these realms or 'information centres' of story operate and weave together, we can learn how to move perspectives, unravel scripts, instigate healing movements and bring meaningful and apt flow into all of our lives.

Welcome aboard! Now let me introduce myself.

The Narrator

I am the narrator and co-navigator (you are the other one!) of this book. A narrator is an important concept, as the narrator simply narrates rather than drives. One of the things that I have found from working with story for many years, is that story is a spirit and if we listen and hold space for it then it can guide us and it can be allowed to flow in a healing way.

I am a narrator for Story. As narrator, I come from the place of Artist, Story Weaver, Visionary Operator, Counsellor and Constellation Practitioner. I will narrate you through the realms of this practice by encouraging each of these aspects in you to come forward and will provide the maps, tools and ideas to inspire and activate these parts.

In turn, the Artist in each us will be encouraged to create and respond; the Story Weaver will be encouraged to listen and to open expressive flow; the Visionary Operator will open up the medicine wheel and invite in the perspectives of the different realms; the Counsellor will hold presence, unconditional appreciation and wonder and finally, the Constellation Practitioner will learn the ways of disentanglement and the power of giving names and places to things to bring freedom and autonomy.

In *Story Compass*, I will narrate and co-navigate with you through a working model that you can explore.

I will introduce you to the Medicine Story Wheel which is guided by the ship's wheel that turns us to each of the directions on our expedition. As we step inside these realms, the Medicine Story Wheel will open. Each of these realms is seen as an influential story field and device.

Alongside the unfolding of the model and the visiting of each of these realms, your lives and the plots within will be happening! I will narrate you through the storms and thickets of the environments and timeframes in your lives as they happen, to be able to enter into the live story fields at work and affect change. This is all live magic at work!

By taking the role as narrator, I can model a way that can

illuminate the choice we have each day to take the conscious narrator role. When I narrate, I acknowledge that there is a narrative at work and by naming myself as such, empower myself to be able to affect the narrative. By the end of the journey, we will each have studied the realms to be able to step into the place of holding an enlightened viewpoint on the narrative. I am trusting that my narrator self here can come from the vision of wholeness that the medicine wheel holds.

Destination

Where would you like the Good Ship Story to take you? If you attune to what stirred you to pick up this book, what do you recall? Or what is true for you now that you are in it?

Take some time to think about where you feel you would like to be after going through this journey. There will be so much more than you know of course too. Captain Columbus set sail for India and ended up in America. So, it might be unimagined and a surprise. But what would you like to be your destination? What is your intention or the calling that has brought you here?

Write your intention down as an affirmation in the present tense, as if you have already reached it and place it somewhere you can see it. Perhaps you will pin the paper and its words to the notice board listed below.

Preparation

Here are some items to collect and prep to go through for your expedition. Take the next bit of time to assemble and set up space. Then you can enter into Direction 1: North and our work with Author will begin.

Items

- Ship's log for taking notes
- A notebook for writing exercises
- Pens and pencils

- Sketchbook for drawing, collage and doodles
- Speaker for playing music
- Walking shoes and waterproof clothing
- A drum or rattle
- The beginnings of a dressing up box and storage for props
- A mapping table and a notice board
- An area for photographs and artefacts for the ancestors
- A recording device for commentaries

Anchor Tree

Find a tree on the land that you can connect with most days. This will be your Anchor Tree and will support you to make a connection with your senses through the four directional realms and to stay in the everyday too.

Connecting with your Anchor Tree

Over the next days, take a walk in your local area and be open to the thought that one of these trees here will be your special tree for this book. See who comes forward! Find out what kind of a tree it is and introduce yourself in your own way. If you are restricted in mobility, ask a tree in your garden or connect with a tree on the land remotely.

So, now find yourself by this tree in person or through visualisation. Take some time to attune and feel yourself with a body separate to the tree's body. Feel the ground beneath you both.

Listen to all the sounds there are around you. With the tree at your back, allow yourself to ground with the world of sound making.

With your eyes, search out all the visual information around you at this moment in time. Be aware of textures and tones. With the tree at your back, allow yourself to settle for a minute or two with the world of visual form making.

With your sense of smell, search out all the scents in the air around you this time. Be aware of sweet and sour. With the tree at your back, allow yourself to ground for a minute or two with the world of aroma making.

With your sense of touch, feel the form of the tree, its branches, bark and the earth you are both on. Be aware of roughness, smoothness and pattern. With the tree at your back, allow yourself to settle for a minute or two with the world of touchable form making.

With your sense of taste, with your tongue taste anything you feel drawn to (that you know is not poisonous of course). Be aware of the flavours. With the tree at your back, allow yourself to ground for a moment or two with the world of flavour-giving.

Now bring attention to yourself as a sensory being in this world. Feel your connection with the world through your senses. Feeling the tree at your back, allow yourself now to connect to the tree as a being. Access a deeper sense to do this. Now feel yourself as a being. Begin to open up to the earth, the sky, the creatures, the grass, all as beings. Stay like this for about five minutes. Feel your everyday self move into a different space from this cool calm clear earth sense of self. You are in the North. Here you are Author.

Now open up to the idea that behind this layer of a realm in the present moment there is the realm of your past. Feel the possibility of everything you have ever experienced being able to be with you and your tree in a long line. Feel this life going deep inside your tree as a vibration of being through time. Stay with presence for this for about two minutes. Here you are in the East. You are Lifeline.

Thank the lifeline and move now to make a space for the ancestors who exist in a realm of time behind this one. Be curious about them and again, let them have a space and a lineage that goes inside the tree in a timeless space. Feel these presences and lives going deep inside your tree as vibrations of being through time. Stay with presence for this for about two minutes. Here you are in the South. You are in the Ancestral realms.

Thank the ancestors and move now to make a space for the archetypes that exist in a realm behind and running through this one that we know as the Mythical. You can include the spiritual dimension of nature in this realm too. Be curious about this realm of Myth and again, let this realm have a space and a lineage that goes inside the tree in a timeless space. Feel these presences and lives going deep inside your tree as vibrations of being through time. Stay with presence for this for about two minutes. Here you are in the West. You are in the Mythical realm.

Thank the realm of Myth and come back to the everyday and your body. Take some breaths. Return to your everyday senses. Notice how present you feel with everything right now.

Now bring out the intention you have made for *Story Compass*. Read it out loud and feel yourself being honoured in this place with the intention you are holding. Just simply be with the tree, soul to soul. See what thoughts and senses you have. Over the next weeks your relationship will deepen and the way you communicate will become clearer.

The Sea

Find a way to bring the sea (your life) into your home. Perhaps it will be a bowl of water on your mapping table; perhaps it will be a photograph or a painting on your notice board; maybe it will be a shell you can hold to your ear to hear the sounds of the sea. Honour the sea as life.

The Ship

Do you have a ship or a boat that you can bring in to be your body? Or perhaps you will choose to put a photograph of you on your notice board to represent you. Maybe you have a puppet that looks a bit like you? Do you have a compass or something that you can have to represent the ship's wheel?

A Map

The map will be your journey to experience and know what the Story Practice is to you. What map will you bring out for this do you think?

Story Practice

For this opening part, as your Story Practice you are going to tune into your life at the moment as sea.

Put on your diver's suit for protection and resourcing. This might be an animal like a seal or a whale that you can merge with, a wet suit with a mask or a bubble of light. Set the intention that your diver suit is equipped with plenty of oxygen and also that in wearing it, it sets an intention that you are not available to take on any trauma or baggage from the sea of your life.

Remember my narrator's idea that you are on a study expedition of story to find out what a Story worker is at the end of it. Remember also the personal destination and intention that you are bringing along.

Now go in there, to your life, as if swimming into the sea. Let it become an amorphic field to you. Pen in hand or keyboard in front of you, begin to write: 'My life the Sea'.

What is in there? How does it feel? What do you notice? What is the story field like? How many different realms can you perceive in there? How many Authors can you perceive in there? How many lifetimes? What ages can you tap into? What characters from Myths or legends, religions or stories do you bump into? Write, write, write.

After your swim, climb out from the sea. Find yourself back on land. Say thank you to everything and close the door on this experience. Have a cup of water, rattle or smudge with a herb (this can help clear your aura to come back to your self clearly again). Feel your feet on the earth. Put away what you have just written to pick up and look at with eyes anew tomorrow.

In a moment, I will talk you all through the then chartered

territory for Author. Please know that the structure for each direction will follow the rhythm of Anchor Tree, Sea, Ship, Map, Story Practice and Excavations and Findings as chapters. It is recommended to take a week for each. If you do this then each direction will last six weeks and the overall book material will cover six months of your life. But go with what feels good for you!

Bon voyage!

Direction 1: North (Author)

Narrator

Hello, this is Narrator speaking.

Today we set course for the North!

Remember how in the Story Wheel model, each of the four directions North, South, East and West relates to the story information held by the physical body, the vibration of the lifeline, the lives of the ancestors and the dimension of Myth that are the planes behind this one respectively?

Well, each of these places in time, space and then beyond does inform and affect the lives we individually live and the story fields we operate inside! So, we will head off in turn to each direction to visit these four information centres. Right now, we are heading off on a voyage into Direction 1.

Cast a gaze up at the position of the Pole Star and then at your map to ascertain North. Move your hands on the ship's wheel to decisively steer your ship onto a Northerly path. We head for territory where we are able to examine and study the subject of and the information held by you, the Author.

The meaning of Author allegedly is from the old French 'auctor or acteor' which means originator, creator or instigator. Earlier it was from the Latin 'acteor' meaning something like promoter, producer; builder, founder; trustworthy writer, Authority; historian; performer. You can see how active, involved and effective the Author is. Author is literally 'one who causes to grow,' as the agent noun is from auctus, past participle of augere 'to increase', and from the PIE root 'aug' 'to increase'. How powerful is that? Consider yourself the powerful Author of your life!

In the North, we are entering into the story fields as experienced and directed by self. We will be exposing the self who resides in your physical body as an unconscious agent complying and colluding with the perpetuation of certain scripts that might not necessarily be for the best interests of the individual.

We will also bring through the self in the light of a conscious agent who can work effectively with changing scripts to bring the self to an empowered and creative place. We will call these two parts the Secret Author and the Empowered Author. But now, before we go any further, let's ask a couple of questions:

What is Story?

Story at its most pragmatic means 'a connected account or narration of some happening'. It is from Old French estorie, estoire, meaning 'story, chronicle or history'. Late Latin storia was shortened from the Latin historia 'history, account, tale, story.' So, by derivation story is a short history, and by development it is a narrative designed to interest and involve.

The stories of our lives are also the Authorities of our lives. If we can become aware of the stories and their Authors or the Authority we give to certain stories and their Authors, then we start to be able to find ourselves as influential agents again. Often, we find ourselves as Authors playing weak roles or cast into invisible places. This book allows us to explore how story happens and to see how we can become victims of stories sometimes. With awareness and techniques, we can begin to make some helpful changes.

The *Story Compass* ethos holds a visionary map for Story. The visionary way is a holistic lens that includes the many realms beyond the human realm. From a visionary perspective, there is an understanding that nature holds stories and perspectives too. By tapping back into nature and its stories as a resource we are able to restore harmony and wholeness.

By allowing the story of nature to feature centrally again and by accessing this also through the archetypal characters (originally developed from the archetypes of nature) of stories that have been passed down to us (a central character will feature in each quarter), we bring in the power to create change. Story has many layers and many perspectives!

Why are Story workers needed now?

For a lot of humans, it is evident that we live in an entangled world. It can be difficult for some of us to feel in control and to understand what is going on that make it hard to feel like we can be in our own flow.

The natural world we live in is really missed out when we think about living in right relationship with everyone. Human beings have in the main lost the art of and belief in the practice of communicating with other members of the earth community (nature, weather, creatures etc.). Conversation can feel dull and lives only part informed or lived when the magical, the natural and the colours of our wider nature are excluded from showing their presence and their importance. What is more, the craft of the bard and the storyteller and the bringing in of the wealth and the resonance of the ancient handed down stories has been again mainly lost in our societies.

On a more basic scale, there is a growing acceptance and understanding that the stories we tell ourselves can create or change realities and there are a number of therapeutic models that support the claiming of this (e.g., narrative therapy, gestalt therapy, transactional analysis, cognitive behavioural therapy). Spiritual practices featuring the existence of a connection with a wider story via trance and prayer is beginning to show itself more. There has been a growing appreciation of the positive effects of mindfulness and nature especially in therapy and education over recent decades.

The *Story Compass* practice can build on and deepen what is beginning to be heard and allowed again. It has the potential to bring through a model to both undo damaging scripts and empower new ones.

Structure: Realms, Chapters and Roles

You know that there are four directional realms (North, East, South and West) each comprising of six chapters. Each direction has the same structure (Anchor, Sea, Ship, Map, Story Study, Excavation and Findings). The roles and approaches of the Artist, Story Weaver, Visionary Operator, Counsellor and Constellation Practitioner are described and drawn on throughout.

- The Pole Star (the intention you hold) guides the way. In this way, a script will be allowed to flow.
- Realms
- Author
- Lifeline
- Ancestors
- Myth
- Chapters

Anchor

In Anchor you will return to the set up space with your tree and work with the Visionary ethos triangle model. This is nature, knowing and trust with presence in the centre. This practice will help you to get your bearings with the subject of the direction, which for North is Author. Each of these points of the triangle will come alive as character anchors for the Story work to unfold.

Sea

In Sea you will return to the way you have found to bring the sea (your life) into your home.

With a simple exercise (each direction introduces a new method) you will be finding ways to bring your life into view. The methods explored will become tools for possible future Story work.

Your perspective on sailing the sea is your destination direction. For this sector it will be North. So, your life will be studied through the lens of you as the Author. Your journey is steered by the intention you have bought to this book and this is metaphorically, the Pole Star.

Ship

In Ship, we work with a major archetype who becomes the ship's context for the subject. In the North this is Mother Goose. You work with drumming or playing music and simple movement to embody the archetype and become aware of how you stand in the everyday world in the direction we are working with.

The archetype becomes a guide that supports the development of discernment. The ship's archetypal guide Mother Goose later supports the Author, with its Secret and Empowered aspects.

Map

In Map, we work with excavating a map through various mediums. Mapping becomes an aid for allowing what is there to come to the surface. The North has 1. Nature responding; 2. Taking a walk or ride (depending on mobility) and 3. Speaking, as its mediums.

Story Study

In Story Study the task of allowing discernment with story becomes the focus. The Story Practice is with the Secret Author and the Empowered Author. We work with chairs, mats and costume to allow a simple disentangling practice to show its effectiveness. You might also choose to draw or paint this process too.

Excavation and Findings

In Excavation and Findings, you are invited to go back to the ship's wheel, the ethos and the anchor of your tree to make a simple journey to your Author self. You will see what images the Author self has to share to make doodles, drawings and collages in your notebook. You will ask what has become clearer and what you have learnt that can be supportive in your work with others and report back in your ship's log.

The Roles

Each of the following roles of a Story worker will come into play: The Artist in each us will be encouraged to create and respond. The Story Weaver will be encouraged to listen and to open expressive flow. The Visionary Operator will open up the medicine wheel and invite in the perspectives of the different realms. The Counsellor will hold presence and unconditional appreciation and wonder. The Constellation Practitioner will learn the ways of disentanglement and the power of giving names and places to things to bring freedom and autonomy.

The Voyage North

Chapter 1

Anchor

Getting your bearings

Take a moment with your notebook or ship's log to think about your voyage North and a study of story through the lens of the Author.

How are you doing right now as we begin? What is it like in your world today? What kind of state is your life in? What is nature up to? How is your tree? How is the weather as we set sail on our metaphorical journey to the far North?

What does going North conjure up for you? How do you feel about going North? What does it mean to you to be leaving land to go to this new place and to cross an ocean like this? We have six chapters at sea until we find the North spot and take the *Story Compass* flag out onto the land.

When you think about a study of the Author in your life who or what comes to mind? The Author is you, but it is an aspect of you. On this ship that is your body or context, you can relate to the Author as an entity that you carry as a part of you or as an outside force. You are about to set sail with the Author in all of their truth. It is just you and the Author together on board. How intimate and non-distracting!

Who do you see before you as the Author? Is there one or are there many guises that the Author takes? Where does the Author appear in relationship to you? When we talk about the Secret Author, who steps out of the shadows? When the Empowered Author is mentioned, who or what do you envision? Can you feel the potential of great findings from this study of story when we focus on Author? I wonder what the study will bring to shore.

Ethos

Your task this week is to really ground in the Visionary *Story Compass* practice.

The visionary way is to be in a space where we can both be present with what is and also be ready and equipped to be in touch with information and understanding that comes from the bigger picture. In *Story Compass,* this can also be called 'the place that goes beyond all stories.' Being able to be in this space allows impartial listening. It also moves us to a space of being able to divine another way, be open to a kind of grace that can bring ease and all sorts of resolutions and openings. The visionary way is to be in a place that allows the way of intuition. It allows the play of the muse. The muse is the term used in ancient Greece to define the concept of creative inspiration.

Anchoring with a practice that supports us to get into this zone - or 'zen' maybe is a good word for it – (zen means focus and in the moment) is a ground rock for this practice. For this reason, Anchor is repeated with the same formula throughout the book. You will probably notice that you already incorporate many ways of holding this way of being in your life. What I suggest here is just a model, so please, take your own well and trusted ways and at the same time feel free to follow or to be creative with what I suggest. The formula is designed to inspire an opening and not to be a dogma.

In the introductory material, you were guided to set up space with a tree and to begin a practice being present with the tree and be in sync with the rhythm of nature.

In Anchor, you are invited to continue with this practice and get to know the visionary formula I mentioned earlier of presence, knowing, nature and trust.

A simple formula

I have developed the formula from many years of studying and teaching what it is to occupy a visionary space. It begins with the practice of being present. Presence is the first and central principle to begin to come to a place of being impartial and neutral. Then the triangle of knowing, nature and trust are the principles that follow presence.

Try the exercises below to begin to develop a strong relationship with presence, nature, knowing and trust. Over time you will begin to feel that you belong more and more with the realm of nature and the vision and effectiveness of this will become clear to you.

The points of the triangle will come alive as the book introduces them as character anchors to help the Story work unfold.

Presence

Presence is the central pole of the entire visionary practice. It is what runs throughout everything. Presence is the act of being present, of not running away or rushing. It is the act of unconditionally and whilst holding awareness and compassion being able to be present with what is. It is a place of power and courage. It is a place that takes us out of dialogue and duality and into a place of observing and allowing a meeting with the heart of any matter. This is the place where the visionary hangs out. It is a place with no judgment, advice or overlay. My personal feeling of when I get to this place of being able to be present is like the air conditioning comes on. It feels cool and disentangled but very kind and loving also.

Over this time, practice noticing when you are present and when you are in a place different to presence. What does it take to move yourself back to presence again each time you notice you are not present? When do you find yourself most easily present? Make some notes.

Nature

Sit with your back to the tree you have found, or visualise yourself there. Focus on your breath and simply become mindful to what chatter inside your head might be going on. You don't need to push it out. Presence is about allowing awareness to arise and comes from a different place to the mind chatter.

Let yourself move into your senses. Touch - feel the air on your skin, touch the ground with your fingers and the surface of the tree, grass and nature around you. Smell - breath in the scents. Taste - taste the air, lick the grass or bark. Hearing - let your ears take in the sounds. Sight - let your eyes cast on everything as if seeing for the first time. Let nature join you through your senses.

In this space, bring yourself to an awareness of being present and in the moment. You are looking to become present with nature both within and without. Now imagine this presence as being able to exist throughout all times. Take yourself to the beginnings of everything. Feel the origins. Feel the today. Allow a conversation to happen moving with presence with your senses and nature through these two stations of presence.

Bring yourself back. How do you feel about nature now?

Knowing

You will need a frame drum, tambourine or rattle for this task to connect with knowing. Drum beats and rattle sounds help to create a steady sound that helps our brainwaves to slow down to match the wavelength of nature and then to the slower wavelength of sleep. This takes us into the dreamtime and a place of visioning. Drums and rattles are instruments that have been used for thousands of years to create a sacred visioning space, opening up to the realms beyond the everyday. They are powerful members in the long story of opening and accessing story fields!

Pick up your drum or rattle. Visualise a bubble of light

around you that holds presence. Set the intention that you are only available here to connect with your knowing. Choose a colour to coat the bubble around you that sets the boundary that this is a clear space for you. You can extend a second bubble to go all around your home and the boundaries of the land around your home and set the same intention. Sit and connect with being present again.

Now focus on your knowing. Think of a time when you have known something. Commence drumming or rattling. (You will do this for about fifteen minutes.) Connect with your knowing and let all your attention and the attention of the drum beat flow to hold awareness for this knowing.

Ask yourself 'Where does this knowing come from?' Feel the origins and authenticity of your knowing. Let it strengthen and take its place. Observe what happens for you. You can also do this with by playing a drumming track if you don't have a drum.

Come back and thank your instruments and the space that held you. Take some notes.

Trust

Go back to your place in nature. Move into a place of presence. Be in your senses. Take some time to land and be with the earth and the weather. Feel yourself as a part of this wider system. Open up to feeling the interconnectedness of everything. Become aware of each of the different systems within the outer nature that operates right now. Feel how they work together and the plan that they are a part of. Feel into your trust for this plan.

Now feel all of the systems going on within you and your body, mind, emotions, passions. Feel your organs and your blood flow, the beating of your heart, your lungs breathing, your eyes and the way your thoughts respond to your eyes working. Feel how you connect with the outer world through your lungs and your sight and thoughts, your sense of smell and your emotions.

Move back again to your awareness of the systems in nature outside of you and the plan everything including you is a part of. Feel into your trust for this plan.

Spend about fifteen minutes in this being with trust. Come out of the task and then make some notes on how you found this and any insights you had.

Chapter 2

Sea

The Author's Life

Bring in now what you have found to bring the sea (your life) into your home. Remind yourself of the Pole Star intention you have for this *Story Compass* journey. Having the anchor as the first week and the connection to nature as central to this practice means that you have in place a stability and a clear grounding and sure place to go back to with your tree. As we are working with story and opening awareness and understandings in the story of ourselves and the worlds we interact with it is important to take it slowly, make it creative and appealing and also to remember that the first principle of the Author is that we each have the right to decide whether to join in with the play and the project or whether to take time out and sit and anchor with our tree and nature. I recommend going out to your tree every day.

In the sea chapter we set up our space as playwrights! You will need your notebook and your box that you have props inside and the intention to keep on making and collecting props. At sea, this is where your dressing room and stage set design starts to build.

Resourcing

We begin by building resources. I have a phrase in teaching visionary work: 'It is all in the prep!' Healing work can happen because a robust space is set up and we have everything in place for grounding support and deep listening from that which is most able to listen. Things can only safely come out into the light because the space is safe, strong and provides all the resources that are needed.

Below is the first task that the Good Ship Story recommends in the Sea section.

1. Life boats

Connect with knowing. If knowing were to be a character, what character would they be? What would your knowing wear, feel like, sound like or smell like? What would they be called?

Ask your knowing to really tune in and make a list of things you already do or go to that make you happy and keep you in the everyday or be an escapist when the going gets tough. Ask them to add some extras that you know will be good for you to have in there too.

Here are some examples:

- Sit outside
- Meditate
- Watch an uplifting movie
- Shape shift to be sunlight
- Go for a walk
- Get lost in a book
- Dance (make life boat playlists especially for these times)
- Make a nice meal
- Have a hot chocolate
- Go for a run
- Phone a friend
- Visit a special place
- Find water (go to the beach or a river)
- Wear my best clothes

Have a go at your own. Make it your lifeboat list for when the sea gets choppy and the going gets overwhelming. Put down all thoughts of looking for meaning or 'doing the book' when you get to these places.

How do you feel having this list here now? What does it tell you about what is important to you and nourishing for you in your life? How much do you follow your knowing and apply this way of listening to your needs generally? What do you realise about your Author from this task?

2. Life View

In North, the simple exercise and method introduced to bring your life into view is Autobiography Mapping. An autobiography is the story that you tell of your own life.

Take a big sheet of paper and make yourself an island map. This map is to be your stage. On this map make territories for childhood, adolescence and teens, twenties, thirties and upwards (depending on your age!). You might also have areas that are parenthood or where you have worked with a certain role. Start to mark places for these areas of your autobiography where there is treasure. Mark the spots with an X. Then have a think about some of the initiations you might have been on in these times and see if you can find territory names. For example, a series of doomed relationships in the teens or twenties might be 'The Den of Relationship Minotaurs' or a scary and confusing time in your childhood might be 'Helter-skelter of the skeletons'.

What you are doing here is honouring the treasures and then also taking the difficult parts into the realm of Myth. We will look at this more in the West, but basically if we can take our own experiences into the realm of Myth then we can open them up to a perspective and a realm that brings healing energy into the everyday realm. Myth holds the bigger picture as well as the lived experience and so it is able to bring both empathy and resources. That is why story heals. You are bringing your life story in its simple form into a container of Myth so that it can be acknowledged and given the hero or heroine of a story status it deserves!

Try putting your Pole Star intention on the same sheet as the map and see how they sit together.

Play some music. I recommend La Wally by Vladimir Cosma, Eric Satie's Gymnopedies or something moving and strong, without lyrics. Connect with the Pole Star as a place of power and feel it connected with the knowing you have established a link with. Invite the Pole Star to shine down onto your map, bringing acceptance and belonging to all of the stories of your life. Take a step back from your map to a neutral place. See what it feels like to hand over your life to the Mythical and to both the Pole Star and your intention right now.

After the music completes, you can continue by rattling, drumming, singing or sitting in the silence for a while. Thank the Pole star, your knowing and your life lived.

How do you feel now? How is your life in view after this exercise of creating a map for your autobiography? How is the story after bringing in the perspective of the Mythical and the Pole Star and inner knowing?

Creative Theatre

If you were to create a character for Author from the stance you have now, who would that be? How would they dress? See if you can come up with a costume for your Author and over the weeks bring the items for the costume into your costume wardrobe.

What have you learnt about story and your autobiography from this exercise?

Chapter 3

Ship

Who is that flying over across the sky towards us now? She seems to come from the heavens themselves! Is it a bird, a plane, a woman? Ah – it is both bird and woman. It is Mother Goose! Welcome Mother Goose to our ship. Take your place on board with us!

As we put our focus on ship, the physical carrier, the body and self we open our work to meet and learn from this brilliant major archetype who becomes the ship's context for us all. Mother Goose, one of the most important storytellers of all is with us.

As we wait for Mother Goose to take her place with a cup of tea in an armchair, on the starboard side, let me tell you first a little bit about archetypes. Archetypes occupy the realm of Myth and are basically clear forces of expression that come from original creator energy.

Let's imagine life from the beginning of time right through an eternity of darkness, then light and then times when fire and all of the elements slowly came into being. Can you imagine the day that the archetypes must have burst through as expressive forces born of the elements to tell the stories of creation and destruction and the cycles of life? Dragon has been shown to me as one of the very first of these archetypal creatures and guides. It is possibly easy to understand how the gathering and formation of each of the pantheons of Gods and Goddesses through different cultures began. Each deity or esteemed post holder carries archetypal energy pertaining to one of the elements. Did you know that the tarot cards (allegedly sourced in Ancient Egyptian times) with their four suits, major and minor arcanum, are systemic storytellers through the archetypal weave, pulling out the threads and forces of the one whose life is being read by the skilled reader?

As humans, we have relationships with these archetypes. They move through us like chords. Some of them are really strong for us and each of us will find ourselves relating with certain Mythical beings in legends, Myths and fairy stories. Sometimes we can get stuck in a sad story; occasionally certain scripts hound us. At times we seem to get lucky over and over again. Understanding the role of the archetypes and our part in the living of them can really support acceptance of the point of things, the putting of certain stories to rest, empowerment in making changes or moving through story landscapes to embrace a new archetype.

One of the ways that the Story Weaver works is by understanding the need for story to bring context to our jumbled lives. Without story we cannot find our bearings. Equally, caught in a story that doesn't permit us to live our life force, we need another story to set us free. The storyteller will sometimes dig from a vat of stories to find a story that will bring resonance or healing in much the same way as the Pole Star brought Mythical perspective earlier. Other times, the Story Weaver will listen to the story she or he is hearing in the life or community of another and feel into what classic archetype is being played and then bring in an archetype for the person to relate to (as in the Story Study below).

The ancients would act out Myths and stories to their community to allow emotions and understandings of what was happening in the community to be brought to the surface. The comedy and tragedy design of Greek theatre recognised the need for these stories to be injected into the culture. Today we have a great plethora of films we can easily access in that may play the same purpose when prescribed with an understanding of the power of story. Many of us have come across that certain film at just the right time to bring understanding and release in our lives.

The embodiment of certain archetypal characters by actors was also known to bring the energy of the Gods and a clear, freeing archetypal expression into the human layer. Actors would experience a form of enlightenment, which could be in turn conveyed to bring healing (restoration of wholeness) to the community. The actors were like Gods for the people. I guess nothing has changed there in the way we view movie stars and our famous archetypal privileged people today!

With the Story work we are doing in the Ship sections, we invite the embodiment of certain archetypes as characters, landscapes or situations to awaken archetypal strength, or unlock insights in ourselves and the people we work with.

Let's meet Mother Goose!

Mother Goose

Mother Goose, tell us your story.

"Hello. Thank you for having me on board your ship.

I am Mother Goose: the proverbial Author; one of the sources of all the fairy stories that ever passed the lips of old and came to be written in words today. I am as ancient as ancient can be. I can't be dated, though many try to pin down my birth. I am immortal, but swing between the worlds of the realm of Myth and the realm of humans. I know the fairy well and reside with them often. You can read my messages by watching the formations of the feet of geese as they fly. You can call me in to soothe your infants with my tales, though some of my stories will also terrify. I am the keeper of story, the lover of words. I understand the wonder and magic that the container of a story can bring.

Pick up a drum now or put on a music track. Place yourself in front of me and shine with the light of your heart. Ask your heart to spin a protective cocoon all about your body and energetic field. Know that this cocoon will set a signal for safety and allow you only to connect with what is healing and good for you.

Sense me here as you drum or fall into the music. Ask me to let go of my impression, and to be in front of you now as only a clear Mother Goose energy with no form or name. Then, ask me to merge with you and let yourself do the same with me. Embody me, dance me or simply drink of me. Feel how I stimulate and awaken the power of the original Author in you. Let me be with you for ten minutes of your time, drinking my energy deep and allowing it to illuminate the origins of the true Author in you. Only after that time will you let me go and thank me but let the experience of what has been lightened inside you remain and be a glaring truth."

With this, Mother Goose goes back to sit in her rocking chair and sips her tea.

I invite you to make some notes. What did your merging with the original Author bring for your own Author? What is happening for you now? How has the experience of embodying one of the original Authors changed you as the Author? How has this experience of embodying contributed to your understanding of story?

For the rest of this week and in certain situations, choose to reconnect with Mother Goose and merge with her clear energy.

Does this develop your discernment of your Authorship in stories in any way? Notice and take notes on how this affects you and the scripts you are a part of.

Chapter 4

Map

Let's take the Author for a swim in the sea of life that surrounds our ship. You will be taking a walk in your local neighbourhood or beyond, to begin mapping the story of your current lives.

Map will become an aid for allowing what is important and true to the way you live to come to the surface. There are three methods you will employ for investigative Story work: nature responding, taking a walk or ride and speaking.

It's time to jump and start swimming in the sea that is your life!

1. Nature responding

Spend a bit of time swimming around and thinking about something that is bothering you in your life at the moment. It might be a worry, some shock that is in you from an event, anger about something that keeps happening or a feeling of being powerless in a certain situation for example.

On your walk, carry this in your heart and in your body. Bring into your consciousness the fact that you are going to find something in nature to tell your story to. It might be a rose flower, a tree, a blade of grass, a dead log or a twig on a tree, for example. See where you are drawn to and which part of nature calls to you.

Ask the flower or branch 'Is it is ok to tell you the story of what is on my mind right now?' Go elsewhere if you get a no! Then begin to tell. Feel as if this is the only being that exists in the world that is there for you right now as you pour out what is there. Know that telling what is true and authentic in you helps truth and authenticity everywhere and that the nature body you have chosen simply holds the right kind of space for you.

After you are complete, give thanks. How do you feel now? Make some notes.

2. Taking a walk or ride

Think of an area in your life where you feel stuck. Describe your stuckness as a feeling, a shape, a colour and a character. Now set out on a walk or a wheel chair journey if you are unable to walk and ask your walk to be a story that will assist the freeing of the stuckness. Look for signs in the story field of your life as you move around. Make notes of what appears. Collect things that you find. When you come to the end of your walk, have all the notes and objects in front of you and create a 'poem of freeing' from it all.

3. Speaking

You are going to speak gibberish! Gibberish are sounds that come out naturally from the place of your will and imagination, but you have no idea what they mean.

Choose something in your life at the moment to focus on. It can be something troubling or something happy. It can be someone you know or a place or an object. Bring this totally to mind and bring to the fore any of the feelings you have about it. You can have an object that you put in front of you that represents it.

Now speak gibberish to it in an expressive manner for five minutes or more.

How do you feel now? Take notes.

What do these three exercises reveal to you? What do they show you about the relationship with the world around you and your inner Author?

Chapter 5

Story Study

In Story Study, the task of allowing discernment with story becomes the focus. The Story Practice is with the Secret Author and the Empowered Author.

The Secret Author is the part of you that is unconscious and drives scripts. It is so subtle you don't even know it is there yet!

The Empowered Author is the one who is able to work in an inspired and supported way, tapping into the metaphorical and the Mythical to bring positive changes and peace to the story in their lives.

Mother Goose leads this exercise.

Freeing the Author

"Bring some chairs onto the deck. Let's have four of them. One for you, one for the empowered Author, one for the shadow Author and one for me, Mother Goose.

Great. Now let's open the Story Wheel. Pick up your rattle and whistle. You can open space like this before you set up all of your Story Study sessions!

I rattle and whistle. I face and call the North and the Place of the Author and the Keepers of the North, place of the present and the physical realm. You are all so welcome. Thank you for being here.

I rattle and whistle. I face and call the East and the Place of the Life stories and the Keepers of the East, place of the lifeline. You are all so welcome. Thank you for being here.

I rattle and whistle. I face and call the South and the Place of the Ancestral stories and the Keepers of the South the Ancestral banks. You are all so welcome. Thank you for being here.

I rattle and whistle. I face and call the West and the Place of Myth and the Keepers of the West the Pillars of light as archetypal forces. You are all so welcome. Thank you for being here.

I call the centre and know that this is also the circle. A circle of light surrounds this space. An orb of light surrounds this space. This space is a place of wholeness, a space beyond all stories that may contain all that goes beyond what we can ever possibly know.

This space is clear. This space brings deep listening. This space is held by all that is pure and true. This space is open.

Take some time to become present now. Feel a grove of trees all around this space. Feel the knowing inside you listening and holding space with you.

Sit in your chair. Focus on presence. As you do so, take the time to see what comes to surface as the story you bring that is stopping you from sinking into relationship with the present moment. Let your feelings and thoughts take you to where you need to go in this sacred Story Wheel. Feel the orb of wholeness and the grove of trees holding you safely.

Become aware of the seats of the Secret Author, the Empowered Author and I, Mother Goose.

Take some notes on how you feel right now and what is coming up for you.

Now, what you are going to do is to move to each of the other seats in turn and just ask that they bring their information and medicine to whatever you have brought to this meeting with your focus on presence. Spend two or three minutes or more in each seat.

Begin with the Secret Author. What is happening that you never knew before? Sit with the Empowered Author. What does the Empowered Author bring as power for you?

Now to my seat! What comes as medicine for you here?

Return to your own seat. You can take some time now to write a story about this experience, or just let a free flowing story happen. I will wait with you.

And now when you are complete, I say: 'Thank you everything for holding this space.

The space and the Story Wheel session is now released and closed.'"

Narrator

With this, Mother Goose flies away as naturally as she swooped in. Thank you, Mother Goose! Thank you for your wisdom and your ancient holding and story carrying.

What did this exercise show you about the Author?

Chapter 6

Excavation and Findings

We have arrived as close as we can get by sea to the North Pole! It is time to disembark. I see you are dressed in a snow suit. Well done! It is a sunny day. Can you see how low the sun is in the sky here? Come on; get the flag that says Author. Don't worry; it will dissolve into the Mythical again as soon as we leave. Here's the ladder and down we go. Across the ice now with your brilliant snow boots gripping the snow and keeping your feet warm. And look, here is a little igloo for you! Come inside, there is a fire burning and some rugs to snuggle on for a while. Can you press play on the drumming track on the simple device you have in your pocket? Close your eyes now. Listen to the steady beat. You are North. Sink into the North. You are Author. You are in this body and you are in this story of you. Let yourself sink into that. How does it all feel? Is North what you expected?

Take fifteen minutes in this igloo in the North journeying to the Author that is you. Ask the North to bring you any remaining medicine for your journey to be even more the true Author in this cosmic story of which we are a part. Ask the North to bring you guidance and even more understanding about story and the work you will do on the Good Ship Story and beyond. Give the North your intention for this book. Ask them to bring enlightenment for you.

Thank and leave a gift for the North. Leave your flag. Take notes!

Getting ready for the next direction

As you return to the ship and take a shower and redress in fresh, warm clothes, feel the gratitude of this journey North.

You find yourself once again at the ship's wheel. Imagine your tree behind your back. Feel present. Acknowledge knowing as a character and everything that you have found out about Author and Author's part in Story work. Moving out of the icy area takes a while, but eventually you find yourself in a place where there is just sea again all about you.

Soon it will be time to head East. But first, take some time with your Author self and the ship's log. Have a look at what your Author has shared and what they want to share more of now. They may want to create doodles, drawings or put together some more collages in your notebook. Ask your Author self what has become clearer and what you have learnt that can be supportive in your work with others and their Author self. Report it all back in your ship's log.

Direction 2: East (Lifeline)

Narrator

Hello, this is Narrator speaking.

Today we set course for the East!

Remember how in the Story Wheel model, each of the four directions North South, East and West relate to the story information held by the physical body, the vibration of the lifeline, the lives of the ancestors and the dimension of Myth that are the planes behind this one respectively?

Well, we are complete with our time in North now and ready to head off to face an Easterly direction and to visit the next information centre. The Author is conscious. Let us contemplate a voyage into Direction 2.

As with each new turning, cast a gaze up at the position of the Pole Star and then at your map to ascertain East. Move your hands on the ship's wheel to decisively steer your ship onto an Easterly path. We head for territory where we are able to examine and study the subject of and the information held by your very own lifeline.

Fields

Let's firstly consider the subject of fields!

In any story, there are morphic and morphogenetic fields at

work. Morphogenetic fields are immaterial information fields that both influence and determine the form of material things. They store the collective habits of species. Morphic fields in social groups connect together members of the group even when they are many miles apart. They provide channels of communication through which organisms can stay in touch at a distance. It is one explanation for telepathy. Morphic and morphogenetic fields contain the memories and specific energies of both an individual and a group. What an exciting concept to consider! As we work through these next three directions and cover the life lived, ancestral and archetypal story information centres, we have the scope to explore the influence of fields through each of these lenses.

With any story in our lives, we can find a governing energetic force in place that will show itself to us in any moment in the way that a story will unfold. The field will generally orient itself towards the energy that exists in relationships.

Here in the East and in the area of the lifeline, our focus is on the way that morphic and morphogenetic fields are imposed upon our current lives. The fields are built from the happenings and trends we have experienced in all of our previous life events and through all of our relationships. This includes our relationships with people, creatures, groups, organisations, buildings, institutions and both natural and politically orchestrated land allocation.

Working with fields is a bit like having x-ray specs and being able to see clearly the previously invisible threads that magnetise and puppeteer our lives. The freedom to change the points on the tracks of our lives to the direction of the story our souls would choose for themselves becomes possible.

Autoethnography

What is autoethnography?

Autoethnography is more widely known as a form of

qualitative research. As part of a study, a writer will use self-reflection and usually writing, to explore anecdotal and personal experience and then connect this autobiographical story to wider cultural, political and social meanings and understandings.

In the study through the lifeline, we will be bringing in the practice of autoethnography as a loose experiment. With the support of the archetype of this realm - Merlin - and the focus on nature, an appreciation of the wider cultural, political and social influences on our autonomy and visionary nature will come to the fore.

Working with story and different expressions of story, there is a possibility to disentangle ourselves from some overbearing past experiences.

Are you ready? Before we set sail, let's have a look at the course ahead!

The Chapters

Anchor

The practice with the tree and the Visionary ethos triangle will help you to get your bearings with the subject of direction East, which is Lifeline. Nature comes alive as a character for the Story work to unfold.

Sea

In Sea you will return to the way you have found to bring the sea (your life) into your home.

With a simple pictorial exercise, you bring your life into view. Your life is studied through the lens of your lifeline experience and influence.

Ship

In Ship, a major archetype becomes the ship's context. In the East this is Merlin. You embody the archetype to become aware of how you stand in the everyday world in the context of your lifeline. The ship's archetypal guide, Merlin, helps you to develop discernment.

Map

Mapping becomes an aid for allowing what is in the lifeline to come to the surface.

The East has 1. Miming; 2. Multi-sensory and 3. Acting as its mediums.

Story Study

In Story Study the task of allowing discernment with story becomes the focus. The Story Practice is with the Secret Lifeline and the Empowered Lifeline. We work with chairs, mats and costume to allow a simple disentangling practice to show its effectiveness.

Excavation and Findings

In Excavation and Findings, you step onto shore to make a simple journey to direction East. You will ask what has become clearer and what you have learnt that can be supportive and report back in your ship's log.

Roles

Here is a reminder of each of the following roles of *Story Compass* that will come into play. The Artist in each us will be encouraged to create and respond. The Story Weaver will be encouraged to listen and to open expressive flow. The Visionary Operator will open up the medicine wheel and invite in the perspectives of the different realms. The Counsellor will hold presence and unconditional appreciation and wonder. The Constellation Practitioner will learn the ways of disentanglement and the power of giving names and places to things to bring freedom and autonomy.

The Pole Star guides the way. Remind yourself again of your intention and adjust it if the North has opened more clarity or vision. In following the Pole Star and your intention, a script is allowed to flow.

The Voyage East

Chapter 7

Anchor

Getting your bearings

The ship is released from its mooring. Take a moment with your notebook or ship's log to think about your voyage East and a study of story through the lens of the lifeline.

So, first of all, how are you doing right now as we begin? What kind of state is your life in? What is nature up to? How is the weather as we set sail on our metaphorical journey Eastward-bound?

What does traveling East conjure up for you? How do you feel about going East? What does it mean to you to be heading off to this new place and to cross an ocean like this? We have six weeks at sea until we find the East spot and take the *Story Compass* flag out onto the land.

When you think about a study of the lifeline you have lived how does that feel? We are really going into the realm of memory here! What does opening memories bring up for you? Are you feeling excited, worried, pulled back or with a bit of trepidation as you anticipate a journey into your past? The lifeline is your lived story so far and as such impacts on the life you have ahead of you. But it is only an aspect on your life because you are coloured by it. On this ship, that is your body or context, you can relate to your lifeline through a body that has lived through all of this. You can carry the weathered aspect of your ship as part of you or as the product of an outside force. You are about to set sail with your ship of life in all of what it knows, breathes and resources you with. It is just you and the story of your life together on board. How intimate and non-distracting!

What do you see before you as the lifeline story to open? Where does the lifeline appear in relationship to you? When we talk about the Secret Life, who steps out of the shadows? When the Empowered Life is mentioned, who or what do you envision? Can you feel the potential of great findings from this study of story when we focus on your lifeline? I wonder what the study will bring to shore.

Ethos

Your task this week is to really ground in the Visionary *Story Compass* practice. Remember that the visionary way is to be in a space where we can both be present with what is and also be ready and equipped to be in touch with information and understanding that comes from the bigger picture.

In Anchor, you are invited to continue to set up space and practice being present with a tree to allow yourself to be in sync with the rhythm of nature tin order to acclimatise yourself with a way of working and holding yourself.

A simple formula

Remember, the formula begins with the practice of being present. Presence is the first and central principle to begin to come to a place of being impartial and neutral. Then the triangle of knowing, nature and trust are the principles that follow presence. Continue the exercises below to begin to nurture your relationship with presence, nature, knowing and trust.

Presence

Presence is the central pole of the entire visionary practice. Over this time, practice noticing when you are present and when you are in a place different to presence. What does it take to move yourself back to presence again each time you notice you are not present? When do you find yourself most easily present? Make some notes.

Nature

Sit with your back to the tree, or visualise yourself there. Focus on your breath and simply become mindful to what chatter inside your head might be going on. Presence is about allowing awareness to arise and comes from a different place to the mind chatter.

Let yourself move into your senses. Touch - feel the air on your skin, touch the ground with your fingers and the surface of the tree, grass and nature around you. Smell - breath in the scents. Taste - taste the air, lick the grass or bark. Hearing - let your ears take in the sounds. Sight - let your eyes cast on everything as if seeing for the first time. Let nature join you through your senses.

In this space, bring yourself to awareness of being present and in the moment. You are looking to become present with nature both within and without. Now imagine this presence as being able to exist throughout all times. Take yourself to the beginnings of everything. Feel the origins. Feel the today. Allow a conversation to happen moving with presence with your senses and nature through these two stations of presence.

Bring yourself back. How do you feel about nature now?

Knowing

You will need a frame drum, tambourine or rattle for this task to connect with knowing.

Pick up your drum or rattle. Visualise a bubble of light around you that holds presence. Set the intention that you are only available here to connect with your knowing. Choose a colour to coat the bubble around you that sets the boundary that this is a clear space for you. You can extend a second bubble to go all around your home and the boundaries of the land around your home and set the same intention.

Now focus on your knowing. Think of a time when you have known something. Commence drumming or rattling. (You will do this for about fifteen minutes.) Connect with your knowing and let all your attention and the attention of the drum beat flow to hold awareness for this knowing. Ask yourself 'Where does this knowing come from?' Feel the origins and authenticity of your knowing. Let it strengthen and take its place. Observe what happens for you. You can also do this with by playing a drumming track if you don't have a drum.

Come back and thank your instruments and the space that held you. Take some notes.

Trust

Go back to your place in nature. Move into a place of presence. Be in your senses. Take some time to land and be with the earth and the weather. Feel yourself as a part of this wider system. Become aware of each of the different systems within the outer nature that operates right now. Feel how they work together and the plan that they are a part of. Feel into your trust for this plan.

Now feel all of the systems going on within you and your body, mind, emotions, passions. Feel your organs and your blood flow, the beating of your heart, your lungs breathing, your eyes and the way your thoughts respond to your eyes working. Feel how you connect with the outer world through your lungs and your sight and thoughts, your sense of smell and your emotions.

Move back again to your awareness of the systems in nature outside of you and the plan everything including you is a part of. Feel into your trust for this plan.

Spend about fifteen minutes in this being with trust. Come out of the task and then make some notes on how you found this and any insights you had.

Chapter 8

Sea

The Life lived

Let's return to what you have found to bring the sea (your life) into your home. Remind yourself of the Pole Star intention you have for *Story Compass*. Having the anchor as the first week and the connection to nature as central to this practice means that you have in place a stability and a clear grounding and sure place to go back to with your tree. As we are working with story and opening awareness and understandings in the story of ourselves and the worlds we interact with it is important to take it slowly, make it creative and appealing. Something to remember is that with the focus on our own lifeline comes the natural premise that we each have the right to take ownership and responsibility for our individual life and life force. You are in charge of your choices - no one else! This means you can decide what you are in a place to do. You can choose whether to bring your life's material to the play and the project or whether to step back and simply be present in the now (e.g., sit and anchor with our tree and nature).

I recommend going out to your tree every day and keeping connecting with presence. As much as we are on a study of story and how it works, we are ultimately living our lives.

In the sea work we set up our space again as playwrights! You will need your notebook and your box that you have your dressing room inside and the intention to keep on making and collecting props and costumes

Resourcing

Once again, we begin by building resources. Healing work can happen because a robust and safe space is set up. This means that we have everything in place for grounding support and deep listening from that most able to listen. Things can only safely come out into the light because the space we create is caring and strong whilst providing all the resources that are needed.

1. Life boats

Connect with nature as part of the visionary triangle. If nature were to be a character, what character would they be? What would nature wear, feel like, sound like or smell like? What would they be called? Make some notes!

As you open up to nature all about you now, ask your true nature to really tune in and make a list of those things that help you to be in tune with nature and have nature and the natural cycles as a dependable base. Ask your true nature to add some extras that you know will be good for you too.

Here are some examples:

- Embrace weather
- Stomp on the beach with the waves
- Lie on grass and merge to be grass turf
- Make songs for the trees
- Put my ear to a tree's trunk and listen to the tree
- Plant seeds
- Water the plants
- Let my hands get in the soil
- Pick berries
- Go on a walk to identify trees
- Go foraging
- Climb a mountain
- Get up when the sun rises
- Do yogic salutations to the sun every morning

Make your own nature lifeboat list for when the sea gets choppy and the going gets overwhelming. Make it your go-to. Put down all thoughts of looking for meaning or 'doing the book' when you get to these places.

How do you feel having this list here now? What does it tell you about what is important to you and nourishing for you in your connection to nature in your life? How much do you apply this way of listening to your needs generally? What do you realise about your lifeline and your connection to nature in your life lived from this task? Are you able to feel the pulse of your lifeline coming through yet?

2. Life View

In East, the simple exercise and method introduced to bring your life into view is autoethnography mapping. An autoethnography studies how your own story is impacted by a wider ethnographic story.

Take a big sheet of paper and write down the title 'Fields of Influence'. Think about your Empowered Author that you have located in your work with North. Ask your Empowered Author to be an overseer and a protector for you with this piece of work.

Take a rattle that you can rattle as you tune into this exercise. Or, you might choose to play a drumming track instead. I recommend you spend ten to fifteen minutes in the following task.

Feel a protective pale blue orb all around you. Set the intention that you are held in a soothing, loving and watery light that can cleanse and keep you connected to love as you work through this. If at any time the exercise becomes too intense, then simply feel yourself going back to that pale blue light and come out of the exercise. You can go back in when you feel calm or ready.

Please also set the intention that you are only available to connect to what you feel ready to open to. Know that you are the one in charge here and if you feel yourself go somewhere that is overwhelming, then let your Empowered Author know you need them to stand between you and what you are encountering and gently bring yourself out of the task and bathe in the pale blue.

Imagine your special tree behind you, grounding you and holding a space to take away anything that you can now release and bring in extra earth energy as is needed. You could also choose to do this outside with your tree wearing earphones.

As the drumming plays, or as you rattle, open up to connect with the earth beneath you, your tree and feel yourself grounded and held. Then, open to be aware of your own body's energetic field. Feel the physical, emotional, mental, passionate and different spiritual expressions of you as a field. You might also include your chakras in this with your base chakra the physical, your sacral chakra the emotional, solar plexus the passionate, heart chakra the mental and then your throat, third eye and crown the ethereal, astral and stellar spiritual expressions. Let your self take time to connect with each of these. After two or three minutes, you will possibly feel like your aura is a glowing field of radiating energy. Feel the power of this.

You are now going to imagine your life lived so far. Tune into the idea that you in this place right now in your current story is affected by the life you have lived. Feel your life around you as the circle of your life lived from conception until the present moment. Take some minutes to honour this. This is your creation and your experience. How cool and amazing is that?

Take some time to let your lifeline land. In your own time, ask to become aware of some of the fields that have influenced your life. To give some examples, this could include family fields; the field of intimate relationships; the field of dreams and ideas you have borne; the field of dreams borne by others for you; the field of different institutions you have studied, worked or been involved with and it could be the field of land where you have lived. Keep open to seeing what is there. Know that the job is to simply see them there and honour their presence. You might bow to them, showing you mean no harm.

After you feel complete, bow to everything and let your Empowered Author know that you are ready to disconnect now. Allow the fields to dissolve. Move back to feeling your own field shining brightly and then moved back into feeling at home in your physical body. Thank your tree and everything for holding space for you.

Reach over to the paper you have set aside with the title 'Fields of Influence'. Make a shape for 'you' in the centre of the paper. Be immediate with your charting now! Try not to think too much about it, but with different colours of pencils or pens, begin to draw some shapes for the different fields you have met in the exercise. Label them so you can remember what they refer to. Take your time but work intuitively and without questioning yourself.

On completion of this task, take some time to study what you have drawn. Notice how the fields overlap and how big or small they each are. Think about the significance of the colours you have chosen for each or patterns you have drawn within them. Notice how close or far away from you each of them has been positioned.

Are you surprised by what has come up here? Does marking them down in this way change the way you view your own story at all? Make some notes.

Sit in the silence for a while. Thank the Pole Star, your true nature and your lifeline for all that they hold.

Creative Theatre

If you were to create a stage set or a terrain that would be the lifeline from the stance you have now, what would that be? If there were significant props and tools what would they be?

See if you can come up with a stage design for your lifeline and some props and tools showing your working with some of the fields of your life. Over these weeks bring the items for the stage set into your stage and props department.

What have you learnt about story and what is coming up as autoethnographical themes from this exercise?

Chapter 9

Ship

We have a new guest on our ship right now: A guest who with the help of his great magic has come through time to be here today. Merlin the Magician, you are so welcome! Take your place on board with us!

As we put our focus onto ship, the physical carrier, the body and the liver of your life, we open our work to meet and learn from this brilliant major archetype that becomes the ship's context. Merlin the Magician, shape-shifter extraordinaire is here to guide us. He wanders over the deck and nods to us, holding a curly hazel staff in his right hand.

Merlin has found a table at the stern of the ship and is setting up an arrangement of artefacts on its surface. Can you see? He has placed a velvet blue cover as a tablecloth. On it he has placed crystal balls, scales, stones, feathers, bags of herbs, some cards with images painted onto them and a stack of golden discs.

Can you remember what was written about archetypes when we began in the North? Archetypes occupy the realm of Myth and basically are clear forces of expression that come from original creator energy. If you would like a memory jog, revisit the Chapter 3 Ship in Author.

Remember that with the Story work we are experiencing in the Ship sections, we invite the embodiment of archetypes as characters, landscapes or situations in order to awaken archetypal strength or unlock insights in ourselves and the people we work with.

Merlin is very much the Magician archetype and the communicator of nature. We work with Merlin as the archetype of the Magician but also the landscape of Merlin's story as the fundamental archetype of nature and wildness. Can you feel your magical nature and wild spirit rising to the occasion? I hand over the narrator role to Merlin!

Merlin

Merlin, tell us your story!

"Hello and thank you for having me on board your ship. I am Merlin the Magician. According to legend, I lived a life in times gone by. Right now, I live in the spaces in-between. My time on this plane was in the twelfth century in the castle and courts of Camelot where I was King Arthur's advisor, prophet, magician and friend. Many ask did we, the members of the story of Camelot actually ever exist or are our stories fictional? I ask the same of you and everything that you bring to the table of your lifeline right now!

I am Merlin. I lived to be able to hold an understanding of the mysteries of life and to exist as a seer and a visionary. My teacher was nature. I have a story to bring through to you on the ship you sail of a time in my life when nature brought through everything for me. I hope it will be of assistance to you on your own journey of opening and attuning to the wilder force of truth that you are. Sit comfortably in this seat here. Here is my tale to tell.

My story begins at a point after my long and dreadful flight from a scene of devastation.

At last, I am far from battle. By some miracle, I have survived and escaped the terrible scenes of death and killing and the chase of many agonising spirits. The sounds, visions and memories of all that I have fled from still clings on and weighs hard on my soul. For hours, have I wandered deep into this forest to be finally daring to imagine that I can be safe. I feel empty, traumatised and disillusioned. I want to never have to set my eyes on the disappointing form of a member of humankind again. Why all this war? Why all this base and unimaginative level of existence? Surely, we are better than this? So many I love, left as dead. So many I have grown up with, left fighting for values I cannot support.

I find an oak tree: A trusty, sturdy oak. I wrap my arms around its form and gain sustenance from its energy for a while. I step back to examine the beaten armour I am wearing. I see the bloodstains of the boy who was in my care, who will never laugh, question, or challenge me again. I fight back fiery tears to furiously dig a hole with my bare hands. I strip off the armour and my clothes to bury all. Following this, I must have fallen into a fitful, nightmarish sleep for I awake naked and cold, recalling dreams of the souls of those I left behind, being called by the ancestors to move from this world into the next. Their moans of release and despair have wrecked my soul even more by the time morning comes.

I awake to the plain truth that I have no idea where I am. My run from the world of men and women was an unendurable plight to freedom. I couldn't retrace its path if I wanted to. I decide that my life from this point forward is to be alone as a hermit here in this wood.

I have all the skills to live this way. I kill a deer. In the next hours I create clothes from its hide. I build a shelter. I pick food from the forest. I make and build fires. I find myself living in a kind of trance. I feel spirits pleading and speaking with me, but I have no interest in anything except surviving and I trust nothing.

As weeks go by, I come to more of a centred place. I realise that the spirits who call me are only looking for guidance and answers, so I help them. After a time, the voices quiet, the wood stills and I hear the gentle, loving whisper of trees. I become receptive to the interconnected communication system of life forms in this woodland. I steadily fall into a pace with this world of peace and harmony. My place in all of this becomes clear. In time my interactions with all of the creatures and trees, the clear sensed wisdom of the ancestors, the interchanging scenes of the weather spirits and the appearance of stars and passage of the moon are imbued with synchronicity and meaning. I finally feel what it is to belong in this realm of earth. The dogmatic training I have undergone as a Druid bows in reverence to this new position. Everything I am learning now comes directly from the spirit realm and as such is untainted and pure. I let go of the horrors of my life as a warrior and with this any ideas of what it was to be my former self. So dissolves forever the bridge to my previous existence.

One day, a little pig walks into my life. This creature becomes a wise and playful companion to me. I spend much time with my new friend, following him through the woods and listening to his stories. One day, the pig sets off and leads me to the orchard of apples. It is on a little island accessible by a raised path on the river. This orchard becomes my sanctuary place.

After a few times visiting the orchard with pig, I become aware of a presence. I catch a glimmer out of the corner of my eye. Then I feel I hear someone calling my name. Over time, I see a feminine form weaving through the trees, every day getting closer. Until one day she approaches me and speaks.

I cannot understand the words. Her language is strange and ethereal, more like the rustling wind. I listen in captivation to the sounds. Over the days and weeks that I visit and spend time here, her language becomes clear to me, as what she speaks reaches deep within. I realise now that these sounds are meant for me. She speaks of the folly of man and how people are cutting themselves off from this realm, from the sacred teachings of the pure ones and the wisdom of ancestors. She tells me how people have forgotten how to get back to this place. She shows me the source of the stories of manipulation of time and energy and the diversions to fear, greed and ignorance. She affirms what has turned me away from the world of humans to come here. But the orchard lady's words are also illuminating into the cause of disrepair and violence. With a shock I come to realise that what she is leading me to is the realisation that it is my role to help repair the bridges back to the pure ones. My journey into this place and this land has brought me a light and a reconnection. The shining ones of nature are longing to reconnect the people back with this too. I need to go back to humankind.

The thought of returning sends me into deep depression. I lift my gloom by listening to simple stories in the comforting whispers of the trees. I take to sitting by running water and feeling the power of the rushing, healing, ever moving molecules. I resolve inside myself to stay here. It seems my visits to the island and the orchard are less needed now. My pig takes me on other trails instead.

One afternoon before dusk, I hear an enchanting sound coming from a place in the forest. Whilst staying carefully hidden, I follow the notes that come to my ears to find a man sitting by a fire. He is playing the most beautiful instrument whose sounds are at one with the notes of this place. The chords seem to emanate the voices of the trees. What is this new harmonic that brings such peace and remembrance? I stay hidden in the trees, careful to be soundless. The man leaves as night began to fall, and winds back through the trees, only to return the next day.

For some reason, I keep going back there to sit silently in the trees close to the spot by the fire and to be with the man who plays these blissful notes on this instrument with strings.

One day the man begins to use his own voice to bring sounds and words along with the music. I have forgotten the language of my people, so long is it I had been here in the wilds. But the sounds begin to reconnect with the part of my brain I thought I had surely left behind with the armour and clothes I had buried beneath the oak tree the day I had vowed never to return to the world of men and women.

And then I remember: My sister Gwedydd. The man sings of her love for a brother and great worry. Her wish to see me, her brother again is the most poignant calling of her heart. He sings of how our people need me, Merlin and of how my place is waiting for me. The words of this minstrel, the message from the orchard lady and the longing of this place and all its spirits and communication systems to reconnect with the world of humans again all come together within me. My sister has sent this man out to find me and to remind me of my calling in the world beyond this place. I know without doubt that it is my time to return.

I go to sit by the fire. My sister's messenger jumps to see me in my wild state, but then calms and smiles, in the realisation that I am who he comes to find. He puts down the instrument that I now recall to be a harp. He packs it away and stands waiting for me to follow.

With tears of immense gratitude and surrender, I say goodbye to my faithful friend the pig and all who live in this place that has been my opening to who I truly am. I follow the steps of the one with the harp and the song, back to the land of humankind and to the hope that my return can help my people to open to this same knowing too.

Thank you for hearing my story. Take some time to let it land in you.

Pick up a drum now or put on a music track with sounds of the forest. Let the story I have just told sink even deeper within. Come stand by me at my table carrying these objects and this magic. Feel your heart shining the opening and the remembrance of the magic that has awakened in you from the listening to the words I have shared. Ask the energy of magic in your heart to spin a protective cocoon all about your body and energetic field. Know that this cocoon will set a signal for safety and allow you only to connect with what is healing and good for you.

Now feel me here as you drum or fall into the music here in this landscape of the woods lived in for so long. I am going to let go of my impression now. I can be in front of you only as a clear Merlin energy with no form or name. As you allow this energy to open without a form, remember I am awakened by the world of nature. Ask this awakening to the world of nature energy to merge with you and let yourself do the same with me. Allow this energy to awaken what is natural and connecting with nature that is within you. Feel how I stimulate and awaken the power of the original life-liver in you. Let me be with you for ten minutes of your time, drinking my energy deep and allowing it to illuminate the origins of the liver of true life force life that you are. Only after that time, will you let me go and thank me but let the experience of what has been lightened inside you remain and be a glaring truth."

Merlin stands back, observes and supports as the energy you awaken to be with, inspired by Merlin and this story, opens new pathways. After this piece of work is complete, he goes back to his table and moves around some of the objects.

Narrator

I invite you to make some notes. What did your merging with the one who is awakened by nature do for you as the liver of life? How has the experience of embodying the understanding one of the ways of nature changed your perspective on your life story lived so far and the exercise with the fields? Have any of these fields lost their hold? How has this experience of embodying contributed to your understanding of story?

Has the support of this story, the Archetype of this realm - Merlin - and the focus on nature, allowed an appreciation of the wider cultural, political and social influences on our autonomy and visionary nature to come to the fore? If so, what are you able to grasp about these elements?

For the rest of this week and in certain situations, choose to reconnect with clear energy of Merlin or the awakening with nature and merge with this. Does this develop your discernment of the story fields around you in anyway? Notice and take notes on how this affects you and the scripts that have influenced you or that you are a part of. Remember the part of the story when Merlin buried his armour and clothing with the oak? Remember how he left that life behind? Are there any aspects of your old clothing and life that you are sensing you are leaving behind or that you feel you are ready to leave behind?

Chapter 10

Map

Let's take your life for a swim in the sea of life that surrounds our ship! So, you will be going into your life lived, to begin mapping the story of your life. There are three methods you will employ for investigative Story work: miming, multi-sensory and acting.

1. Miming

The part that over-rules
Before you begin this study, spend a bit of time swimming around and thinking about what systems at play in your life have an influence on the way you behave. What limits your expression? Examples of some of these are: patriarchy; ancestral expectation; society's rules; class systems; racially discriminating systems; science and rationale brain emphasis; political parties; wartime mentality; antiquated Victorian systems; adult-centred vision etc.

Perhaps you can pick up a rattle and set the intention to see these or other systems at play. Ask your own heart to find out which one would be most beneficial for you to explore in this exercise.

Once you have located what you are going to work with, allow yourself to stand and embody the energy of this. When you feel like you really have a sense of how it feels, begin to put the feel of this into movement. Mime the energy of this system at work. Mime it until you feel you have really given it form and expression.

The idea is that by miming it, you are able to discern it and release it from having so much of a hold on you. When you feel complete, come back to a still standing position and then remember you are in sea. Have a good cleanse and wriggle to release.

After you are complete, give thanks. How do you feel now? Make some notes.

2. Multi-sensory

The part that is switched off

You are going to experience nature with the intention of opening up your senses in a new way. Find a spot in nature that you know well (not by water or a drop in height, for safety reasons) and then sit down by a tree there. Put on a blindfold and allow yourself to explore this place with your sense of touch, hearing, smell and taste. Spend about fifteen minutes in this space of opening and exploring. Then remove the blindfold.

Take some time to make some notes. What did you manage to access that is usually switched off in this exercise? What was different about this space to usual? How do you think it would be to spend a whole night in this place? Now you have located this part, how can you begin to open up the part that is switched off more in your everyday life?

You can later choose to do this activity with your ears blocked and see what you access without your sense of hearing.

What have you learnt about your relationship with nature and with your life that has previously been hidden after this activity? What can you do to deepen your connection now?

3. Acting

Appreciating different lenses

Choose paragraphs to read from the Merlin story above as if you are one, two or all of the following. You will need to power up and get into the field (drum or rattle and open the Story Wheel) so that you are genuinely coming from a place of being this representative and not acting in a stereotyped or detached way. You might choose to work with costume to support you too.

- Prime Minister
- Doctor
- Herbalist
- Fairy
- Someone with bipolar-disorder
- Someone with autism
- Someone who is highly anxious
- Member of the Royal family
- Soldier
- Young Offender

What happens when you have spoken the story in the field of these different perspectives? Do you feel any different? How does it change the story? Do you access anything about yourself previously hidden? Does anything surprise you?

What do these three exercises reveal to you? What do they show you about the relationship with the world around you and your own lifeline? How do they inform you about the place of nature?

Chapter 11

Story Study

In Story Study the task of allowing discernment with story becomes the focus. The Story Practice is with the Secret Life and the Empowered Life.

The Secret Life is the life you are living that is unconscious and drives scripts. It is so subtle you don't even know it is there yet!

The Empowered Life is the life that is true for you. It is able to tap into the metaphorical and the Mythical to bring magic and alchemy to other parts of your life.

Merlin leads this exercise.

Freeing the Nature Life

"Bring some velvet cloths onto the deck. You can find them in a pile under my table. Let's have four of them. One is for you, one is for the Empowered Life, one is for the secret life and one is for me, Merlin.

Spread them out like little islands and like story fields. Wonderful.

Now let's open the Story Wheel. Pick up your rattle and whistle. You can open space now, just like you did in the North and before you set up all of your Story Study sessions!

I rattle and whistle. I face and call the North and the Place of the Author and the Keepers of the North, place of the present and the physical realm. You are all so welcome. Thank you for being here.

I rattle and whistle. I face and call the East and the Place of the Life stories and the Keepers of the East, place of the lifeline. You are all so welcome. Thank you for being here.

I rattle and whistle. I face and call the South and the Place of the Ancestral stories and the Keepers of the South the ancestral banks. You are all so welcome. Thank you for being here.

I rattle and whistle. I face and call the West and the Place of Myth and the Keepers of the West the Pillars of light as archetypal forces. You are all so welcome. Thank you for being here.

I call the centre and know that this is also the circle. A circle of light surrounds this space. An orb of light surrounds this space. This space is a place of wholeness. It is a space beyond all stories and contains all that goes beyond what we can ever possibly know.

This space is clear. This space brings deep listening. All that is pure and true holds this space. This space is open.

Take some time to become present now. Feel a grove of trees all around this space. Feel the knowing inside you listening and holding space with you.

Stand on your velvet island. Focus on presence. And as you do so, take time to see what comes to surface as the story you bring that is stopping you from sinking into relationship with the present moment. Let your feelings and thoughts take you to where you need to go in this sacred story Story Wheel. Feel the orb of wholeness and the grove of trees holding you safely.

Become aware of the velvet islands of the Secret Life, the Empowered Life and I, Merlin.

Take some notes on how you feel right now and what is coming up for you.

Now what you are going to do is to move to each of the other velvet islands in turn and just ask that they bring their information and medicine to whatever you have brought to this meeting with your focus on presence. Spend two or three minutes or more in the field of each island.

Begin with the Secret Life. What is happening that you never knew before?

Sit with the Empowered Life. What does the Empowered Life bring as power for you?

Now to my island! What comes as medicine for you here? This can be your opportunity to bring healing to something in your life story too.

When you feel you have a sense of what you have been able to *access, return to your own velvet square. Write a story about this experience or just let a free flowing story happen.*

I will wait until you have completed writing. One you are complete, I say: 'thank you everything for holding this space. The space and the Story Wheel session is now closed.'"

And with this, Merlin takes the velvet squares and carefully folds them. He moves across to the table and tidies away his wares. He picks up the hazel staff he arrived with. He smiles. His eyes twinkle with tree magic. Then he dissolves into thin air.

Narrator

Thank you, Merlin. Thank you for your nature knowing and for your access to magic and the true pulse of life.

See if you can make some more notes. What did this exercise show you about your lifeline and the influence of the Secret and Empowered Lives? What do you need to do now to complete? Is there anything you need to do to make some changes in your life or to help you to remember something important to carry forwards?

Chapter 12

Excavation and Findings

We have travelled as far to the East as we can! It is time to disembark. I see you are dressed with your safari hat and sandals on, ready to move onto land. Well done. It is a rainy day today. Can you smell the scents in the air that the rain brings? Come on. Get the flag that says Lifeline. Don't worry. It will dissolve into the Mythical again as soon as we leave. Here's the ladder and down we go.

Let's cross the pavements now. It looks like we are on the outskirts of a small town. There are people scattered around with their lives to live too! And look, here's a little temple for you to visit!

You have to go over a little bridge over water to enter the temple. Hold tight to the sides. It is slightly shaky as you walk. What an ornate door, look! It is slightly open. Come inside now. Gentle music is playing and incense is burning. The ceiling is high and painted gold. What a beautiful vibrant and colourful place. How prettily it is decorated. It is truly a feast for the eyes!

There are lots of different areas in this temple. Have a look around. Search for that little alcove that is just for you. It will be with a bamboo blind covering the door that you will have to draw open and then close again on entry. You will see candles burning brightly inside this alcove just for you and hear plainly the sound of a harp playing. Is it Merlin's messenger's harp? Ah yes - the world of nature is coming through now into this room. Here we are.

There is a couch to lie on, look, with some cushions. Make yourself comfortable. Close your eyes. Let the harp music take you into your nature life and into the place of East. You are East. Sink into the East. You are the lifeline. You are your lifeline and you are in this story of you. Let yourself sink into that. How does it all feel? Is East what you expected?

Take fifteen minutes in this Eastern temple journeying to the lifeline that is the intelligence of all the time you have lived through being in this life. Enter the areas of your autoethnographic study that have been powerful for you in this section. Ask the East to bring you any remaining medicine for your journey to be even more able to free your life to be your natural way of expressing in this cosmic story of which we are a part. Ask the East to bring you guidance and even more understanding about story and the work you will do on the Good Ship Story and beyond. Give the East your intention for this book. Ask them to bring enlightenment for you.

Then, at the end of your journey with beautiful forest harp music or drumming, thank and leave a gift for the East. Leave your flag. Take notes!

Getting ready for the next direction

As you return to the ship, take a shower and then redress in dry clothes, feel the gratitude of this journey East. And find yourself now once again behind the ship's wheel. Sense your tree behind your back. Feel present. Acknowledge nature as a character and everything that you have found out about the lifeline and a life lived and their parts in Story work.

Moving out of the harbour and this estuary here takes a while, but eventually you find yourself in a place where there is just sea again all about you.

Soon it will be time to head south. First, take some time with your lifeline and the ship's log. Feel your lifeline as the continuum that it is. It is your story, a wealth of substance and embedded connection with the story of humankind and nature. Can you see just how much being in this life and continuing this lifeline with awareness and responsibility is a place of power and effectiveness? How brilliant that you can take the learning from Author and Lifeline to meet the ancestral stories. Have a look at what your lifeline has shared and what it wants to share more of now or how it would like to summarise. It may want to create doodles, drawings or put together collages. Ask your lifeline what has become clearer and what you have learnt that can be supportive in your work with others and their lifelines. Report it all back in your ship's log.

Direction 3: South (Ancestors)

Narrator

Hello again! This is Narrator.

Today we set course for the South!

Remember how in the Story Wheel model, each of the four directions North South, East and West relate to the story information held by the physical body, the vibration of the lifeline, the lives of the ancestors and the dimension of Myth that are the planes behind this one respectively? So, here we are with North and East behind us, ready to head off to face a Southerly direction and visit the next information centre. The Author is conscious. The Lifeline fields have been illuminated. Let us now contemplate a voyage into Direction 3.

As with each new turning, cast a gaze up at the position of the Pole Star and then at your map to ascertain South. Move your hands on the ship's wheel to decisively steer your ship onto a southerly path. We head for territory where we are able to examine and step into the subject of and the information held by your ancestors.

Fate

Let's firstly consider the subject of fate! In Greek and Roman Mythology, there are three goddesses who preside over the birth and life of humans. In these times, each person's destiny was thought of as a thread that was spun, measured, and cut by the three Fates, Clotho; Lachesis, and Atropos. These fates affected the course of a life and then were met, healed and understood.

You can see from the personifications here, that the fates are active and destiny is in fact something that is innate. The fates affect the thread or line of destiny.

In systemic constellation practice the term fate is used widely, considering the impact of the 'fates' of the ancestors, on the thread line of destiny of subsequent family members. Therefore, the three fates include some of the ancestral elements we each 'fatefully' carry through. Constellation work is a therapeutic model that allows the ancestors and their stories to show their place in an individual's current story. By setting up a mini theatre space for this, entanglements with the fates of our ancestors can be picked out either by people physically representing the ancestors to reveal hidden stories in the field, or by the placing of models that the client-individual then intuitively senses for. Once the stories we are entangled with are visible, they can be handed back and forever unmeshed from the story of the enquirer-individual's life.

As far as I can understand, the phenomenological lineage of Systemic or Family Constellation work traces back to philosophers like Franz Brentano, Edmund Husserl and Martin Heidegger. In the late 1960's, Virginia Satir's 'Family Sculpture' and then 'Family Reconstruction' methods brought in the idea of having human representatives to explore a family story. Thea Schönfelder developed Satir's ideas. Bert Hellinger was one of the main practitioners to take these ideas forward. Hellinger merged his experience of living in the midst of an ancestral revering Zulu culture in Nigeria with a Gestalt therapy practice. But it was the Psychotherapist and founder of the School of Individual Psychology, Alfred Adler who first used the term family constellation.

In South, as we sail with the ancestors, we will begin to see and understand how these fates can affect us. We will find creative ways to free ourselves to live more of our own true stories and destinies.

Character

What is character?

In Middle English, character comes from the Old French caractere. The Latin word comes from the Greek kharaktēr that means 'a stamping tool'. Wow! How strong is that? Our character is 'stamped upon us'. You can already begin to see what potential fun lies ahead with the story journey thinking about and tracking the origins of this metaphorical stamping tool!

Our characters are often stamped upon us from ancestral archetypal overlays. Working with story and extending the story fields we learnt about in Lifeline to include the ancestral story fields, all sorts of influences on our character can be found. Character becomes something that claims us or sometimes protects us. Sometimes, this can be fun and interesting and quite useful for us and we want to keep this part of our character. Often, this can be something hugely unconscious and difficult to fathom. In the constellation sessions I hold, I see all kinds of character traits dissolve once they have ben sourced through a past family story.

In South, we look at character closely and find another lens to free our right to live our true stories.

Are you ready to go South now? Before we set sail, let's have a look again at the course ahead!

The Chapters

Anchor

In Anchor, you will return to the set up space with your tree and work with the Visionary ethos triangle model of nature, knowing and trust with presence in the centre. Trust will come alive as a character anchor for the Story work to unfold.

Sea

In Sea, you return to the way you have found to bring the sea (your life) into your home. You honour sea as life. With a simple drawing exercise, you find a ways to bring your ancestors bearing on your life into view.

Ship

In Ship, we work with the Prince from Sleeping Beauty as a major archetype. You work to embody the archetype and become aware of how you stand in the everyday world with the ancestral influences. Sometimes, parts of the stories these characters come from become an environment for the study of the story field in the quarter and dimension. Here it is the bramble hedge that the Prince has to break through to get to the Princess that is the feature we focus on.

Map

In Map, we work with excavating a map. The East has 1. Writing; 2. Drawing and 3. Listening and responding, as its mediums.

Story Study

In Story Study the task of allowing discernment with story becomes the focus. The Story Practice is with the Secret Ancestor and the Empowered Ancestor.

Excavation and Findings

In Excavation and Findings, you go ashore to make a simple journey to the caravan of your ancestry and meet the power of South. You will ask what has become clearer and what you have learnt that can be supportive and report back in your ship's log.

The Roles

So again, here is a reminder of each of the following roles of the Story Worker that will come into play.

The Artist in each us will be encouraged to create and respond. The Story Weaver will be encouraged to listen and to open expressive flow. The Visionary Operator will open up the medicine wheel and invite in the perspectives of the different realms. The Counsellor will hold presence and unconditional appreciation and wonder. The Constellation Practitioner will learn the ways of disentanglement and the power of giving names and places to things to bring freedom and autonomy.

The Pole Star (the intention you hold) guides the way. Remind yourself again of what this is now and adjust it if the North and East have opened up more clarity or vision. In following the Pole Star and your intention, a script will be allowed to flow.

The Voyage South

Chapter 13

Anchor

Getting your bearings

The ship is released from its mooring. Take a moment with your notebook or ship's log to think about your voyage South. Prepare for a study of story through the lens of the ancestors!

So, first of all, how are you doing right now as we begin? What is it like in your world today? What is nature up to? How is your tree? And how is the weather as we set sail on our metaphorical journey Southward-bound?

What does travelling South conjure up for you? How do you feel about going South? What does it mean to you to be heading off to this new place and to cross an ocean like this? We have some time at sea until we find the East spot and take the *Story Compass* flag out onto the land.

When you think about ancestors, what happens within you? Does anyone appear in your mind's eye? How do you feel about the idea of there being a realm where all the ancestors can be reached? Is it easy for you to include the ancestors of the humans and the ancestors of all beings?

On this ship that is your body or context, you can relate to your ancestors through a body that is a product of your ancestral lines. You are about to set sail with your ship of life with all that is in the story lines of the ancestors behind you. It is just you and the stories of your ancestors together on board. It could get pretty busy on board this ship!

What do you see before you as the ancestral realm? Where do the ancestral banks appear in relationship to you? When we talk about the Secret Ancestor, who steps out of the shadows?

What is the atmosphere like when the ancestors are given the space to be? When the Empowered Ancestor is mentioned, who or what do you envision? Can you feel the potential of great findings from this study of story when we focus on the ancestral influence? I wonder what the study will bring to shore in six weeks' time.

Ethos

Your task this week is to really ground in the Visionary *Story Compass* practice. The visionary way is to be in a space where we can both be present with what is and also be ready and equipped to be in touch with information and understanding that comes from the bigger picture.

In Anchor, you are guided to continue to set up space with your tree and practice being present with the tree to allow yourself to be in sync with the rhythm of nature. This will help you to acclimatise to a way of holding yourself.

A simple formula

Once more, we begin again with the practice of being present. Presence is the first and central principle to begin to come to a place of being impartial and neutral. As you know, the triangle of knowing, nature and trust are the principles that follow presence.

With Ancestors, it is the trust point of the triangle that we encourage to come alive as the content develops as a character anchor to help the Story work to unfold.

Presence

Presence is the act of being present, of not running away or rushing. It is the act of unconditionally and whilst holding awareness and compassion being able to be present with what is. It is a place that takes us out of dialogue and duality and into a place of observing and allowing a meeting with the heart of any matter. This is the place where the visionary hangs out. It is a place with no judgment, advice or overlay.

Over this time, practice noticing when you are present and when you are in a place different to presence. What does it take to move yourself back to presence again each time you notice you are not present? When do you find yourself most easily present? Make some notes.

Nature

Sit with your back to the special tree or visualise yourself there. Take some time to become present. Focus on your breath and simply become mindful to what chatter inside your head might be going on.

Let yourself move into your senses. Touch - feel the air on your skin, touch the ground with your fingers and the surface of the tree, grass and nature around you. Smell - breath in the scents. Taste - taste the air, lick the grass, bark, a flower. Hearing - let your ears take in the sounds. Sight - let your eyes cast on everything as if seeing for the first time. Let nature join you through your senses.

In this space, bring yourself to an awareness of being present and in the moment. You are looking to become present with nature both within and without. Now imagine this presence as being able to exist throughout all times. Take yourself to the beginnings of everything. Feel the origins. Feel the today. Allow a conversation to happen moving with presence with your senses and nature through these two stations of presence.

Bring yourself back. How do you feel about nature now?

Knowing

Pick up your drum or rattle. Visualise a bubble of light around you that holds presence. Set the intention that you are only available here to connect with your knowing. Choose a colour to coat the bubble around you that sets the boundary that this is a clear space for you. You can extend a second bubble to go all around your home and the boundaries of the land around your home and set the same intention. Sit and connect with being present again. You will get to know what this feeling is like the more that you practice these concepts of being.

Now focus on your knowing. Think of a time when you have known something. Begin to drum or rattle. (You will do this for about fifteen minutes) Connect with your knowing and let all your attention and the attention of the drum beat flow to hold awareness for this knowing. Ask yourself 'Where does this knowing come from?' Feel the origins and authenticity of your knowing. Let it strengthen and take its place. Observe what happens for you. You can also do this with by playing a drumming track.

Come back and thank your drum and the space that held you. Take some notes.

Trust

Go back to your place in nature. Move into a place of presence again. Be in your senses. Take some time to land and be with the earth and the weather. Feel yourself as a part of this wider system. Feel how they work together and the plan that they are a part of. Feel into your trust for this plan.

Sense all of the systems going on within you and your body, mind, emotions, passions. Feel your organs and your blood flow, the beating of your heart, your lungs breathing, your eyes and the way your thoughts respond to your eyes working. Feel how you connect with the outer world through your lungs and your sight and thoughts, your sense of smell and your emotions.

Move back again to your awareness of the systems in nature outside of you and the plan everything including you is a part of. Feel into your trust for this plan. Spend about fifteen minutes in this being with trust. Come out of the task and then make some notes on how you found this and any insights you might have had.

Chapter 14

Sea

Ancestral Life

Let's return to what you have found to bring the sea (your life) into your home. Remind yourself of the Pole Star intention you have for this Story work. As we are working with story and opening awareness and understandings in the story of the worlds we interact with and ourselves, it is important to take it slowly, make it creative and appealing. Something to remember is that with the focus on our own lifeline comes the natural premise that we each have the right to take ownership and responsibility for our individual life and life force. You are in charge of your choices - no one else! This means you can decide what you are in a place to do. You can choose whether to bring your life's material to the play and the project or whether to step back and simply be present in the now (e.g., sit and anchor with our tree and nature). I recommend going out to your tree every day and keeping connecting with presence.

In the Sea work we set up our space again as playwrights! You will need your notebook and your box that you have your dressing room inside and the intention to keep on making and collecting props and costumes

Resourcing

Once again, we begin by building resources. Healing work can happen because a safe, accepting space is set up. Things can only safely come out into the light because the space we create is caring and strong whilst providing all the resources that are needed.

1. Life boats

Connect with trust. If trust were to be a character, what character would they be? What would trust wear, feel like, sound or smell like? What would they be called? Make some notes!

As you open up to trust all about you now, ask trust to really tune in and make a list. Make a list of things that help you to be in tune with your trust and to feel in tune.

Here are some examples:

- Take deep breaths and remember the universe has a plan
- Go and stand with an oak
- Dance to some slow music and come into my body (e.g., Existence by Hafez Nazeri)
- Practice abdominal breathing
- Learn to play a musical instrument
- Do some balancing yoga positions like Tree Pose
- Read an autobiography by someone who has moved through something (e.g., In Good Timing by Peter Caddy; A Long Walk to Freedom by Nelson Mandela)
- Walk a line
- Set up a still life and draw it
- Colour in a mandala
- Go on a mindfulness walk in nature
- Walk barefoot around the house and
- Run with the wind!
- Write a list of what I trust
- Fill a large frame with photos of my ancestors
- Draw my family tree

Have a go at your own. Make it your trust lifeboat list for when the sea gets choppy and the going gets overwhelming. Make it your go-to. Put down all thoughts of looking for meaning or 'doing the book' when you get to these places.

How do you feel having this list here now? What does it tell you about what is important and nourishing for you in your connection to trust in your life? How much do you follow your trust, apply this way of listening to your needs generally? What do you realise about your ancestral lines and your connection to trust in your life lived from this task? Are you able to connect and feel the pulse of your ancestors coming through yet?

2. Life View

In South, the simple exercise and method introduced to bring your life into view is a study of fates.

Take a big sheet of paper and write down the title 'Fate lines'. Think about your Empowered Author you located in your work with North. Ask your Empowered Author to be an overseer and a protector for you with this piece of work.

Take a rattle that you can rattle as you tune in to this exercise. Or, you might choose to play a drumming track instead. I recommend you spend ten to fifteen minutes in the following task.

Feel a protective pale blue orb all around you before you start this piece of tuning in. Set the intention that you are held in a soothing, loving and watery light that can cleanse and keep you connected to love as you work through this. If at any time the exercise becomes too intense, then simply feel yourself going back to that pale blue light and come out of the exercise. You can go back in when you feel calm or ready.

Please also set the intention that you are only available to connect to what you feel ready to open to. Know that you are the one in charge here and if you feel yourself go somewhere that is overwhelming, let your Empowered Author know you need them to stand between you and what you are encountering and gently bring yourself out of the task to bathe in the pale blue.

Imagine your special tree behind you, grounding you and holding a space to take away anything that you can now release and bring in extra earth energy as is needed. You could also choose to do this outside, with your tree, wearing earphones.

As the drumming plays, or as you rattle, open up to connect with the earth beneath you, your tree and feel yourself grounded and held. Then open to be aware of your own body's energetic field. Feel the physical, emotional, mental, passionate and different spiritual expressions of you as a field. You might also include your chakras in this with your base chakra the physical, your sacral chakra the emotional, solar plexus the passionate, heart chakra the mental and then your throat, third eye and crown the ethereal, astral and stellar spiritual expressions. Let your self take time to connect with each of these. After two or three minutes, you will possibly feel like your aura is a glowing field of radiating energy. Feel the power of this.

You are now going to imagine the caravan of your ancestral lines. First of all, you will need to politely ask permission. Just open up to the idea of connection and honour the ancestors letting them know that you would like to connect with them and that you are coming from a space of non-judgment and unconditional love. The ancestors belong with you, but sometimes there can be programmes of non-inclusion. Calling in a template of unconditional love and understanding can open doors. You can visualise a guide that holds unconditional love like Raphael or Panda or whoever appears when you ask who might be a Keeper of this for you. Let them take a place holding the space with you. Then wait to feel the energy move. Sometimes this can happen instantly. Sometimes it will take a couple of minutes. I have found that in time, the energy will ripple in a refreshing or opening way and then I will know that it is ok to begin. Be gentle with yourself and know that this work can be tender. If you feel it is overwhelming, then ask your guide of unconditional love to shine light into places, feel the Empowered Author standing between you and what you feel the overwhelm with and feel the tree balancing and grounding you. You can also choose to do this activity step by step if it feels like that would be easier for you.

If you are adopted or don't know one of your parents, then you can make a space for the birth ancestors known or unknown and then for the adopted parents and both lineages. Feel behind your right shoulders your father or fathers, and then make a space for his father and mother father at the right shoulder mother at the left. Then know that all of the paternal ancestors can then take their place as a snake of life force - and character.

Now do the same behind your left shoulder for your mother or mothers and for her parents and then beyond. Feel your snake of life force - and the character here too.

Just be with this sense of life force and character flowing right back through the paternal and maternal lines. Notice any points that attract you. What do these attractive points feel like? Do you feel similar to them or like they understand you in some way for example? Are there any heavier areas? What happens in your body when you feel these heavier areas? Now be curious to feel if there are places that feel a bit blank or unreachable. What happens when you notice these patches?

Keep on weaving with your Empowered Author and the Unconditional love guide, letting them go to the places that are needed. Know that the Empowered Author supports you to stand your ground and not get pulled into the stories that are there.

Next, tune into the idea that you in this place right now in your current story is affected by the fates of some of your ancestors. As in the East, feel your life around you as the circle of your life lived from conception until the present moment. Take some minutes to honour this. This is your creation and your experience. How cool and amazing is that?

Take some time to let your lifeline land as a long and wide road in front of you that has brought you to this current point. Stare forwards as if you can see in the far distance the place of your conception and then birth. Then in your own time, ask to become aware of some of the fates of the ancestors who are behind you that have influenced your life. Simply feel the space of your life as a wide road in front of you and then turn around to face your ancestors. Ask four of your ancestors who have a bearing on your fate to show themselves in the road of your life now behind. Keep open to feeling where they go. Know that the job is to simply to allow what has been affecting you to reveal itself and to honour its truth. You can bow to them to acknowledge the gravity of this. It is often that we follow our ancestors out of loyalty and love.

Rattle or drum to allow the fate of the ancestor and your own fate to separate now. See the guide of unconditional love holding space and dissolving any welding.

After you feel complete, bow to everything and let your Empowered Author know that you are ready to disconnect. Turn back around and let your ancestors who showed themselves in your lifeline know they can all move behind you again. See the road of your life in front of you. Allow the fields to dissolve. Let go of your ancestors whilst honouring them and knowing that they are there for you. Move back to feeling your self in the present moment without those fates being carried now shining brightly. Come back into a space of feeling at home in your physical body. Thank your tree and everything for holding space for you.

Reach over to the paper you have set aside with the title 'Fate Lines'. Trace the undulating form of your life road on the paper. Now take some coloured pencils or crayons and colour in where you felt the fate of an ancestor overlay yours. You don't need to know too much; it is just the sensing of it that matters. When you have made four colours of shaded spots, sit back and have a look at what you have drawn and mapped. Know that this has been seen and let go of now. But be prepared for some insights and changes in the way your story continues over the next days and weeks.

How do you feel now? Make some notes. Sit in the silence for a while. Thank the Pole Star, your true nature and your lifeline for all that they hold.

Creative Theatre

If you were to design a coloured lighting and a musical instrument or a sound for each of these fates that has influenced you, what would they be? If you were to compose a tune, song or a haunting melody what would it be? See if you can create something spontaneously to record on your phone.

Over these weeks bring through some sound effects and lighting ideas that you can introduce to your stage and props department that can create the atmosphere of the character of fates and ancestral influences.

What have you learnt about story and what is coming up as ancestral themes from this exercise?

Chapter 15

Ship

Who is the guest for Direction South, I wonder? He has just climbed up the ladder from a small boat that drew alongside. He seems to be dressed up like a Pantomime character. He is tall and dark. He wears pointed shoes and a distinguished hat. His step is nimble. There is a fine energy that surrounds him, yet his cloak is tattered and torn and his skin looks ripped. He is bleeding in places. What is it that he carries in his hands? It appears to be a pair of secateurs. Who cuts through hedges and has the appearance of one who has been on a long and difficult journey and yet seems dressed like a pantomime prince? I know who he must be! It is the Prince from Sleeping Beauty. Come and join us Prince, you are so welcome! Take your place on board!

As we put our focus on ship, the physical carrier, the body and the liver of your life, we open our work to meet and learn from a new archetype who becomes the ship's context. Before I hand over to the Prince of the Sleeping Beauty story. I need to share a little from my story over the last ten days. Firstly, I spent a whole day cutting back a hedge and spent the next five days not being able to stand up easily. The Prince and his task came to mind. Then, I went to stay in a holiday cottage for my partner's birthday and there I found a spindle such as the one used in the fairy tale, on the landing. Returning home, my partner opened a gift sent in the post to find within a set of secateurs. I love how a story and confirmation of its relevance shows itself in the ordinary lives we live. Look out to see if you find this too!

So here we have him, the Prince of Initiation, the one who understands the call of the Mythical to awaken the sleeping feminine, then break and heal the spells of the ancestors. He comes to the South as our guide. He springs over the deck and bows, holding a sprig of the blackthorn bush in his gloved hand, along with the secateurs.

Our Prince has found a table at the stern of the ship and has put the secateurs and the sprig of the thorny white flowered bush on its surface. Can you see? He sits down now on a high backed chair that has appeared in this spot and pulls out his sword.

Remember, the archetypes occupy the realm of Myth and basically are clear forces of expression that come from original creator energy. With the Story work we are doing in the Ship sections, we invite the embodiment of an archetype as a character, landscape or situation to awaken archetypal strength or unlock insights in ourselves and people we work with.

The Prince is the loyal and noble masculine archetype. He embodies the masculine force that reciprocates the calling and power of the feminine. How apt that he would appear as our guide for this direction of the journey as we appreciate the pulls of our mother, fathers, life donators and all of the ancestral stories of that have brought us into being! We work with Sleeping Beauty's Prince as the archetype of the Prince, but also the landscape of his story as the fundamental archetype of an initiatory journey. The wonders of the initiations of you and your ancestors are about to be invoked.

I hand over the narrator role to the Prince!

Sleeping Beauty's Prince

Prince, tell us your story!

"Hello! Thank you for having me on board your ship. I am really happy to be here. Have you heard the story of the Sleeping Beauty? Some know her as Briar Rose. She is the Princess whose christening party missed to send an invite to the Goddess Fairy of Darkness. She arrived after all the other Goddess Fairies had left their gifts and spells of fortune. In the end, her gift was her presence and the spell she brought was the promise that the princess would prick her finger on a spindle wheel one day and along with the whole of the palace and its lands, fall into a sleep for a hundred years.

Her father, in his fear for this, had all spinning wheels banished from the palace. But one day a merchant from a land far away managed to pass through the gates and brought to the princess a spindle wheel to try. The princess pricked her finger and then, well, you know the rest.

A hundred years later I set off on a long track across the lands. I don't know what possessed me, but I had been feeling lost recently and not happy at all with the fortunes my privileged life had given me. I decided I needed to go off on some kind of a pilgrimage to find something that felt missing. Fortunately, my family understood that this was a sacred calling. I set off on the road with enough money to buy food and take lodgings, as I followed a quest.

Have you ever felt the power of a sacred calling? It nips at you like a crazy dog. It drags your heart around. It aches. It points to something deeply missing inside your soul that needs to be returned.

I followed my gut, and in the end, I was guided to a huge forest of blackthorn hedges. The black stapled branches of the prickly trees and the contrasting white flowers belied to me that there was something beyond them they were hiding. See how torn my cloak is? See these scratches and this dry blood? I am surprised I didn't lose an eye. There was something I needed to find inside this thick forest of overgrowth. I took my sword and I fought my way through. It took a day and a night.

As dawn started to barely break, I had made my way through. I found myself in the grounds of an ancient building. There were people sleeping all around. I shook a couple of them, but they didn't stir. I wasn't surprise to see this scene, for I had felt the power of some strange enchantment at work pushing me back all the way. But for some reason, the power of my sword cutting through the blackthorn forest seemed to have diluted the force of it. The more I carved my way in the less it was an issue. As I walked up the steps into what looked like a castle, I could see a light in a room. And there was sitting the Fairy Goddess of Darkness. She smiled at me. I recognised her as half of my destiny. I was pleased to see her. She gave me a bowl of water that I drank from gratefully. Then she left whilst the dark was still here enough to take her.

Suddenly, I saw the Sleeping Beauty. She was lying in a glass casket. I knew she was the other part of my destiny story. She held the mystery of what would inspire and educate my male soul to be able to reach.

I opened the casket lid. I sat there and stared at her, my heart beating like never before. I took her hand and kissed it. And then she awoke.

With her, the whole palace awoke too. Soon it was busy in there.

She spent the next weeks telling me the stories that the dark nights of a hundred years had brought to her. I collected the resonance with them all in my soul. They awakened the Initiate in me. I knew then that we would live together, she would continue to share her wisdom and I would be in service to allowing the initiations in others too.

So here I am now. I frequently make these journeys across the sea to help the ones who call and who feel their destiny, to dissolve and understand the spells of the ancestors and free the incomplete initiations of our forbearers.

Thank you for hearing my story. Take some time to let it land in you. Pick up a drum now, or put on some sweet court music. Let the story I have just told sink even deeper into your soul. Come stand by me and take my sword in your hands. Feel your heart shining an opening and remembrance of this call to destiny and the unknown that has awakened in you from the listening to the words I have shared. Ask the energy of this destiny in your heart to spin a protective cocoon all about your body and energetic field. Know that this cocoon will set a signal for safety and allow you only to connect with what is healing and good for you.

Now feel me here as you drum or fall into the music and as you hold the sword that can cut through the binds of the past. I am going to let go of my impression now. I can be in front of you only as a clear Prince energy with no form or name. As you allow this energy to open without a form, remember I am awakened by the call of destiny. Ask this awakening to the initiation to merge with you and let yourself do the same with me. Allow this energy to awaken what is the true calling that is within you. Feel how I stimulate and awaken the power of the one who knows truly in you. Let me be with you for ten minutes of your time, drinking my energy deep and allowing it to illuminate the origins of the liver of true call to destiny that you are. Only after that time, will you let me go and thank me but let the experience of what has been lightened inside you remain and be a glaring truth."

The Prince stands back. He observes and supports, as the energy you awaken to be with inspired by the Prince and this story allows an opening. After this piece of work is complete, he goes back to his table, puts his sword back in his strap, fiddles with the secateurs, prunes the singular sprig of blackthorn, then turns around and winks.

Narrator

I invite you to make some notes. What did your merging with the one who is awakened by his initiation and quest do for you? What is happening for you now? How has the experience of embodying the understanding of the ways of initiation and the call of the pulls to what is asleep changed your perspective on ancestral fates and the exercise with the caravan of the ancestors? Have any of these fields lost their hold? How has this experience of embodying contributed to your understanding of story?

Has the support of this story and the Archetype of this realm, the Prince, and the focus on initiation, allowed an appreciation of the fates of your own ancestral lines and their pulls and fates?

For the rest of this week and in certain situations, choose to reconnect with the clear energy of the Prince or the awareness the existence of pulls to healing and merge with this again. Notice and take notes on how this affects you and the ancestral stories and characters that have influenced you. Remember the part of the story when the Prince decided to follow the calling. Remember how nothing else mattered. Are there any aspects of your old character that you are sensing you are leaving behind or that you feel you are ready to leave behind?

Chapter 16

Map

Let's take your life for a swim in the sea of life that surrounds our ship. You will be going into your ancestral plains as you begin to map the stories of your ancestors. There are three mediums you will employ for investigative Story work: writing, drawing and listening and responding.

1.Writing
Inheritance

Freedom Writing

Before you begin this study, spend a bit of time swimming around and thinking about what you might have inherited from your ancestors. This might include personality traits, faiths, fears, phobias, traditions, illness, opinions, political views, grudges, social positioning, limiting beliefs, ideas about self, lack of confidence, arrogance, resentments, loyalties. Make a list.

Now think about some of these things and think about whether you would like to continue inheriting them.

You are now going to try out a method of writing I have called 'Freedom Writing'.

Take a walk to find a tree out in nature somewhere and sit with your tree. Ask the tree if it would mind holding space for you as an ancestral 'freedom writing' tree. Tune into the tree and ask the tree if you can invite it to write through you as a freedom writer to help free you with its words from three of the inherited traits from your ancestors.

You can start with words like: 'I am the freedom writing tree and this what I see. I see…' Keep writing until you have written a short story of understanding, release or freeing that comes from the heart.

Repeat twice more with things from your inheritance list and then thank the tree for its support and for this experience.

When you feel complete, come back to a still, standing position and then remember you are in sea. Connect through the roots of the tree to see and feel the connection with the tree and the sea. How do you feel now? Make some notes.

2. Drawing
Get Knotted

The power of entanglements

Get a rope and make a big, messy knot in it. Now get some drawing materials. Place the rope on a surface. Source a big piece of paper or a sketchpad and some drawing materials. Draw it. Spend a good amount of time to get the details. As you are drawing, allow your mind to go to any knots or entanglements you may feel within your family. Just keep faithfully drawing the knot and be present with it just as it is and be present with what comes to mind. When you have finished your drawing, how do you feel?

3. Listening and Responding
Chair work

Interviewing the ancestors

See if you can find some photos of your ancestors, or if you have one, a copy of a family tree. Make a space in your living or working room with a series of empty seats. Assign a seat for one or more of the ancestors who attract your attention and that you are drawn to. Ask their permission to interview them in the piece of work below.

Make up some questions for your interview. They could be questions like: What would you recommend I let go of now? What parts of me are like you? What do I need to know from you that would help me today? You might also choose to go reflow and to see what turns up in your mind as you interview.

Remember you are listening and responding in this exercise so it will become free flowing as the task deepens.

Open the space as a Story Wheel and connect with a protector. Feel an orb of light surrounding you and set the intention that you are not available to take anything on from your ancestors. After each one, make sure you rattle around yourself and step out of their field, returning dedicatedly to yourself.

Now take your place in the interview seat. Then choose a seat for the ancestor you will interview first. Let this chair become their chair.

Move to sit in their chair when you feel ready and clear. Have the list of questions in front of you. Now ask yourself the questions as if you are the ancestor. Each time you ask the question and listen for the response coming from within, then listen with your own heart. Give space for the answers to be heard by you and sensed into. Only respond when you know you are coming from the heart. You can write down your questions, answers and responses then conversation as it flows. Thank each ancestor in turn as you complete and release the chair from being their chair.

At the end, rattle or drum and feel the ancestors all returning to the realm of the ancestors and feel your self back in this dimension. You may choose to smudge with sage or open a window. How do you feel now after this task?

Chapter 17

Story Study

In Story Study, the task of allowing discernment with story becomes the focus. The Story Practice is with the Secret Ancestor and the Empowered Ancestor.

The Secret Ancestor is an ancestor that you are not aware of who is unconsciously hidden in your life and drives scripts. The Empowered Ancestor is an ancestor in your lines who is a rich resource of understanding and resonance for you. They have a strong storyline and their power can tap deep into the metaphorical and the Mythical. Connecting with them can bring magic and alchemy to your life.

The Prince leads this exercise.

Freeing Destiny

"Bring yourself to this space on the ship if you will. Here are some wooden boxes. I am placing them so that, in a moment, you can stand on them.

Let's open the Story Wheel. Pick up your rattle and whistle. You can open space now, just like you did in the North and East and before you set up all of your Story Study sessions!

I rattle and whistle. I face and call the North and the Place of the Author and the Keepers of the North, place of the present and the physical realm. You are all so welcome. Thank you for being here.

I rattle and whistle. I face and call the East and the Place of the Life stories and the Keepers of the East, place of the lifeline. You are all so welcome. Thank you for being here.

I rattle and whistle. I face and call the South and the Place of the Ancestral stories and the Keepers of the South the ancestral banks. You are all so welcome. Thank you for being here.

I rattle and whistle. I face and call the West and the Place of Myth and the Keepers of the West the Pillars of light as archetypal forces. You are all so welcome. Thank you for being here.

I call the Centre and know that this is also the circle. A circle of light surrounds this space. An orb of light surrounds this space. This space is a place of wholeness. It is a space beyond all stories and contains all that goes beyond what we can ever possibly know.

This space is clear. This space brings deep listening. All that is pure and true holds this space. This space is open.

Take some time to become present now. Feel a grove of trees all around this space. Feel the knowing inside you listening and holding space with you.

Stand on one of the boxes. Focus on presence and the idea of Destiny. And as you do so, take time to see what comes to surface as the story you bring that is stopping you from sinking into relationship with the present moment and your destiny. Let feelings and thoughts take you to where you need to go in this sacred Story Wheel. Feel the orb of wholeness and the grove of trees holding you safely.

Become aware of the boxes in this environment of the Secret Ancestor, the Empowered Ancestor and I, Sleeping Beauty's Prince.

Take some notes on how you feel right now and what is coming up for you. Keep your connection with presence and your own destiny as you move through the following.

Now what you are going to do is to move to stand on each of the other wooden boxes in turn and just ask that they bring their information and medicine to whatever you have brought to this meeting with your focus on presence. Spend two or three minutes or more in the story field of each box.

Begin with the Secret Ancestor. Who is there that you never knew before? Take your time. Take about two or three minutes to tune in.

Take your position on the box of the Empowered Ancestor. What does the Empowered Ancestor bring as power for you and our destiny?

Now to my box! This is the box of the one who knows the way of initiation. What comes as medicine for you and your destiny here? This can be your opportunity to bring healing to something in your *ancestral stories too and to free the space even more for your own destiny.*

When you feel you have a sense of what you have been able to access, return to the wooden box that is for you. Write a story about destiny or just let a free flowing story happen. I will wait here with you until you are finished.

At the end of this time, I thank you everything for holding this space. The space and the Story Wheel session is now closed."

And with this, the Prince moves to pick and stack together the four boxes. He leaves them in a neat pile. Then he bows, strides towards the ladder and makes his way down to his little tugboat and sails away.

Narrator

Thank you, Prince. Thank you for your understanding of initiation and for your access to the mysteries of the masculine and feminine threads, for the knowledge of an antidote to ancestral spells and for the way you show us to follow the path of true destiny.

See if you can make some more notes. What did this exercise show you about your ancestors and the influence of the Secret and Empowered Ancestors? What do you need to do now to complete? Is there anything you need to do to make some changes in your life or to help you to remember something important to carry forwards?

Chapter 18

Excavation and Findings

We have travelled as far South as we can! Some islands of the Southern hemisphere are at the side of us. Closer and closer they become, until we reach a shore. It is time to disembark. I see you are dressed with your woollen jersey and thick boots on ready to travel on to land. Well done. It is a still day today. Can you feel the atmosphere air that this stillness brings? Anticipation is in the air. Come on, pick up the flag that says Ancestors. Don't worry it will dissolve into the Mythical again as soon as we leave. Here's the ladder and down we go.

Across the rough tracks now, there are some paths, can you see them? They seem to lead into a deep forest. It is very green here. There is not a sign of any people. Come and follow this path that leads through the trees. It seems to lead to a bit of a clearing. There is a small rocky hillock to climb. Oh look, there seems to be a cave entrance just ahead of us as we walk up. Let's go inside.

There are candles burning in the cave. It is cool in here, but look there is a wood stove. Its chimney must go up to a hole in the roof that moves to the outside air. There is some timber and dry vegetation to build a fire. Plus, matches! Can you remember how to build it? The thin and easily flammable vegetation in the middle and then build the thin sticks in a teepee design around that. Place a few of the bigger sticks around and across. Keep lots of space for air to move in. Open the vents, then strike the match. Aim for the centre. Gently close the stove door, keeping the vents open until it burns bright and orange.

So here we are in the Cave of South. The fire is burning and the ancestors are here with us. There is a frame drum on the shelf. Can you see it - with a fluffy beater too? Why not pick it up and tap on it with the beater as you stare into the stove's wide glass window front and into the flames. In time you may close your eyes and journey into the place of South and the ancestors. Feel the ancestors as a gathering all around you. As you allow yourself now to become the South, notice who shows up. You are at South. You are the product of all of your ancestors. The drumbeat you play now includes all of the heartbeats that ever there were on this earth. Open now to include the heartbeat of all beings and the whole of life including this earth that has kept on living with the same heart beat all the way through this lineage that finds itself in you.

You are South and the ancestors and you are a part of this ancestral story. Continue to drum and surrender to its beat as it takes you into your place in the ancestral stories and into the place of South. Sink into the South. Feel your self as part of the intelligence of an ancestral continuum. You are with the ancestor's lifeline and you are in this story with them all. Let yourself sink into this fact. How does it feel? Is South what you expected?

Take fifteen minutes in this cave journeying with the ancestors who have breathed this story of creation that culminates in you. Enter the areas of your ancestral exploration that have been powerful for you in this section. Ask the South to bring you any remaining medicine for your journey to be even more able to free your life to be your natural way of expressing in this cosmic story of which we are a part. Ask the South to bring you guidance and even more understanding about story and the work you will do on the Good Ship Story and beyond. Give the South your intention. Ask them to bring enlightenment for you.

At the end of your journey with the beautiful drum by this fire in this sacred cave, put down the beater and pause to feel the silence and the sure beating of your own heart. Thank all of the ancestors and leave a gift for the South before you leave the cave to make our journey back to the ship. Remember to position the flag! Take notes.

When you return to the ship, take a shower and then redress, feeling the gratitude of this journey South.

Getting ready for the next direction

You find yourself now once again at the ship's wheel. Imagine your tree behind your back. Bring yourself to be present. Acknowledge trust as a character and everything that you have found out about that which is ancestral and the ancestor's part to play in Story work.

Moving out of the harbour and this estuary here takes a while, but eventually you find yourself in a place where there is just sea again all about you.

Soon it will be time to head West. But first, take some time with your ancestors and the ship's log. Feel your ancestral story as the continuum that it is. It is your ancestral trail story. As such it is a wealth of substance and connection with the story of origins. Can you see just how much being in this story and continuing this life with awareness and responsibility is a place of power and effectiveness? How brilliant that you can take the learning from Author, Lifeline and Ancestors on to meet the Mythical stories. Have a look at what your ancestors have shared and what they want to share more of now or how they would like to summarise. They may want to create doodles, drawings or put together some more collages in your notebook. Ask the ancestors what has become clearer and what you have learnt that can be supportive in your work with others and their ancestors. Report it all back in your ship's log.

Direction 4: West (Myth)

Narrator

Hello again! This is Narrator.

Today we set course for the West!

First, here is a quick recap on the roles you have been holding with Story work and how they operate.

Story Weaver

To get into the zone of Story Weaver, all you really need to do is to set yourself up just like you have been doing in the Anchor tasks. Get into a place where you are present, and connect with your knowing, trust and your special place in nature. See anyone you are working with having a clear access to all of this too. Open space with the Story Wheel and invite the Story Weavers of all times to also be present with you.

Know that your role is to listen and to open expressive flow. Be aware of how you feel in your body, what you notice is happening for you and how you respond to what another says. Be responsible for this. Own you and your responses. At the same time be ready to be positive, curious and unconditionally accepting of the person with you. Be curious about what you might be picking up from somewhere in their story fields.

Know that you are empowering your own and another's

story to unfold, whilst being responsible for your own. Be aware to keep the two clear. The ability will come with practice.

Visionary Operator

It is the Visionary Operator who understands and is in direct communication with the different realms of the Story Wheel.

As you are holding presence, you will be aware of the physical and what is playing for you as Author, in your body. Then you will be curious to notice what is happening for the Author in the people you hold a space for as you hold awareness for their physical presence.

You will be tracking the lifeline of the other person from conception to now. You will be aware that ancestral influences will also be at play. Finally, you will be seeing the person or people in front of you with their own archetypal strengths and guides and holding space ready for whoever the archetypal holder is going to be. In North, East and South we worked with Mother Goose, Merlin and Sleeping Beauty's Prince. In West it will be Anansi. You could have one of these holding spaces for you, or your own archetypal space holder.

All of the time you will be simply letting your intuition and knowing guide you as you await cues that are given. Know that it is about going slowly.

Artist

Your creativity will just know what to do! Your artist will come up with ideas and flow for courses and material with the stories or themes you choose to go with. You could also try to make a place for your artist when you open up space, to really invite them to come through.

Counsellor

The Counsellor is inherent in the ethos of the Story Weaver. The Counsellor is the listener and the one who feeds back with curiosity, but without overlaying interpretation. Phrases like 'I am wondering if...' 'I think I am hearing...' can help the Counsellor aspect to even more open up the dimensions of the shared Story space.

Constellation Practitioner

In these early stages with *Story Compass* work, it is enough to remember that the Constellation Practitioner simply knows that being entangled in the imprints (remember that stamp of character) of others through living, ancestral inheritance and the force of pre-determined archetypal scripts and Myths is a way of life. It is to know that one of the main tasks of the Story Worker is to help to release the grip of these entanglements. Just knowing that the awareness we bring in through some of the story tasks helps to loosen these grips is sufficient. The space and ethos you work with holds the conditions to allow sensitive openings and freedom. From this process, old stories can be felt, heard and released whilst new stories have space to seed and grow. This is the way of the transformative principle.

A Simple Practice

So, to repeat, all you need to do is set up the space and be aware of these roles. At this level of Story work, what you are doing is simply raising awareness and allowing movements so that we can each come into more of a true place.

Go slowly and gently. The book is designed to help you set up safe space and to have a model to work with (i.e., the Story Wheel and the presence triangle) that is robust and supportive. It is designed to acquaint you with some main archetypes and guides for you to start playing. It is also created so that you can go through the material for yourself to better understand and value the ethos and this way of working.

It isn't a book to teach you how to do it my way (although the Story Wheel is my creation so if you do use it, please attribute that part to me). I hope the book gives you confidence to play, follow your own passion and what you are most here to heal then bring yourself or your own calling into the world in an inspired and confident way.

Going West

Remember again, how in the *Story Compass* model, each of the four directions North South, East and West relate to the story information held by the physical body, the vibration of the lifeline, the lives of the ancestors and the dimension of Myth that are the planes behind this one respectively? As you are finding out, each of these places in time, space and then beyond informs and affects the lives we individually live and the story fields we operate inside!

So, here we are with North, East and South behind us, ready to head off to face a Westerly direction and to visit the next information centre. The Author is conscious, the Lifeline fields have been illuminated and the Ancestral fates have been acknowledged. So, let us now contemplate a voyage into Direction West and the lands of the archetypes.

At this final turning, cast a gaze up at the position of the Pole Star and then at your map to ascertain West. Move your hands on the ship's wheel to decisively steer your ship onto a Westerly path. We head for territory where we are able to examine and step into the subject of and the information held by the place of Myth.

Myth

Let's firstly have a look at what Myth is. I understand Myth as the wider realm and also as a place we can step into at any time. I feel Myth as the place that holds the power of story alongside the truth that we are always living these stories. Myth is more popularly known as meaning a traditional or ancient story. It is true that Myths are deeply rooted in the past and that they keep on running through us. When we work in a conscious way with Myth, we find we have a role of being able to change the Myths too.

In West, we will enter Myth through nature and our dreams

and continue to appreciate just how much presence takes us to those powerful opening places.

Last night I had a dream. I woke up at the point of being found with my partner as stowaways on a boat. We were sailing a long river that took us out West and over through the Western Isles of Scotland. The Western Isles kept on stretching further and further West. The landscape and mountains were becoming more and more magical. I could feel them vibrating and speaking to me. Everything was animated. The spirit of the land was very much alive. I was in ecstasy. Then the Cabin Master found us. Even though he was very kind and sympathetic, we were stowaways and so we had to go back. The whole dream had a feel of the Enid Blyton novels I read when I was a child. Everything was so charming and simple. I wasn't too bothered that we had to go back because I had tasted the magic of those mountains and that land and knew that the connection with that meant more than any ticket for a boat. The magic mountains would get me there.

It was only when I was recounting the dream to my daughter over coffee later, that I realised the dream was about going West and its significance to my being in the midst of writing this part of the book. What a brilliant omen!

It was Myth and the magic mountains that brought me to Scotland. When I was at Jacob Kramer College of Art in my hometown of Leeds, on my Foundation Year in the 1980s, Richard De Marco, the co-founder of the Edinburgh's Traverse Theatre come to do a talk. His talk was about Magic Mountains and Myth. I wrote my Foundation year thesis all about Magic Mountains and pledged to live in Scotland one day. I was nineteen. Eight years later, I had come to the end of my time in England and said to my friend, I think I will live in Edinburgh next and then go and live in the Mediterranean. Well, a few weeks after saying this, I flew to Thailand for a holiday and on the way back the plane was so delayed that we missed our connection in Romania and were given visas to go and stay in Bucharest overnight. I hadn't planned this! I suddenly knew with a flash that some plot twist thing was going on. Well, there I met a man under a chandelier in the old communist hotel foyer we had all been accommodated in for the night who seemed to be a mine of information about what was going on. I decided to stick around him, as he was helpful and kind. Back home, he was studying at the Edinburgh College of Art and living in the Fringe city. I ended up following him there.

The next time I met Richard de Marco I was taking my MFA at Dundee University. Richard took us on a Mythical tour of Scotland, introducing us to many sites. That guy is half man half Myth. He has since popped up in my life from time to time like the many other Mythmakers.

Anyway, I haven't made it to live in the Mediterranean yet. But I do dream of Mount Olympus from time to time. So, living Myth is about opening doorways and accessing a magical world within this one, you see.

Archetype

We have been working with archetypes as the guides for each direction. Let's have a closer look at archetypes. An archetype is a clear strong force linked to the power of creation at the beginning of time. Each archetype has a strength. Each also links with an element.

In the dream recounted above, I was the archetype of stowaway. My finder was benevolent but not helpful in getting me there. So, I needed to call on the power of Myth to overcome that part of the story (i.e., the secret stowaway script). Going deeper into the archetype of stowaway might show me more about who I am currently as I am going West. West helps us to see the archetypal roles we are playing and to dip into the Mythical to heal them. We can find Mythical power in the land at any time.

In West, as we sail with the archetypes, we will begin to

see and understand how we weave with Myth all of the time. We will find creative ways to open up to live more of our own empowered nature. In West, we work closely with archetype and find ways to inhabit and help others to inhabit and understand our true range of archetypal natures.

Theatre

The original theatres of the world were also places of healing. My sense is that the ancients understood that life is a playing out of Mythological patterns that are held in the archetypal patterns in the other realms. Both humans and the creator beings hold imprints that act out certain storylines and dynamics. Theatre was understood as a way of reading these patterns and shining the healing light of awareness and attention on to what was being played out and also as a result of seeing this, what needed to be played out as a way of restoring balance.

Theatre would also heal when the energy of the Gods and Goddesses and the primal forces of life could be embodied and brought through into this realm. The actors and actresses could be imbued with powerful energy and this would be transmitted to the audience.

For the ancients, Myth was life. Things weren't as separate. The audience would also participate in the drama as a way of interacting with and empowering their role in being able to help the Myth. The conversation went both ways.

Theatre could also heal by staging events and relationships that would inspire the people to remember and focus their attention on where it was needed. It was a way of educating the emotions to release stored up material and restore hope and a sense of purpose.

We can liken a lot of this theory to the way that children play when left to be in the theatre of childhood. There is a school of thought which advocates that if we allow children to freely act out (with clear boundaries of not really hurting anyone!)

archetypal dynamics in childhood, this helps them to grow up to be more centred and confident adults.

In West, we enter more clearly into the concept of theatre as a place where we can consciously interact with the Mythical in the everyday.

Play

Play is essential to everything! We play and we are in a play. The word play means movement. It is essentially about flow. To play is to flow. To show a play is to show the flow.

As I mentioned above, as children we are perhaps allowing the flow and playing out of certain archetypal movements that need to be expressed. When I co-designed (with Cathy Bache) the curriculum for the Secret Garden Outdoor Nursery in 2007, the ethos was developed very much from the premise of understanding this possibility. We provided a space in nature that had the reverence of being sacred ground for these recently birthed humans entering the cosmos.

As adults, we have grown through initiation to be able to hold awareness and responsibility. With these qualities of awareness and responsibility added to play (for those of us who keep or are able to return to playing), we are equipped to engage with all sorts of wonderful things in the field of creation. This act of engaging with the field and playing consciously is known as art. The artist interacts with the interface of creation and life and has the power to influence the stories of the world.

Before we properly set sail for West, let's have a look again at the course ahead!

The Chapters

Anchor

In Anchor, you return to the set up space with your tree and work with the Visionary ethos triangle model of nature, knowing and trust with presence in the centre. Each of the points of the triangle have already come alive as character anchors for the Story work to unfold now. So, we move to the centre of the triangle for West. We allow Presence to surface as a character.

Sea

In Sea you will return to the way you have found to bring the sea (your life) into your home (e.g., bowl of water on your mapping table; photograph or a painting on your notice board or wall or a shell you can hold to your ear to hear the sounds of the sea). How about revisiting your Sea area and replenishing what you have now, before we sail West?

There is a simple exercise opening to myth to bring your life and its plays and theatres into view. Your life will be studied through the lens of the Mythical influences on the land where you live.

Ship

In Ship, we work with a major archetype that becomes the ship's context for the subject. In the West this is Anansi the Spider from Caribbean folklore. You are invited to embody the archetype and become aware of how you embody your mythical self in the everyday world. Anansi helps you to develop discernment.

Map

We excavate a map through various mediums. Mapping becomes an aid for allowing what is there to come to the surface. The mediums for West are 1. Vision tracking; 2. Mapping and 3. Movement.

Story Study

In Story Study the practice is with excavating the Secret Archetype and the Empowered Archetype. We work with costume to allow a simple disentangling practice. You might also choose to draw or paint this process too.

Excavation and Findings

In Excavation and Findings, you step onto shore and meet the West. On your return to ship, you see what images your own Mythical perspective has to share to make doodles, drawings and collages in your notebook. You will ask what you have learnt on this journey and report back in your ship's log.

The Roles

The roles of the Story Worker, revisited in the opening to West, will come into play.

The Pole Star (the intention you hold) will continue to guide the way. Adjust it if you have found that the North, East and South have opened up more clarity or vision. In following the Pole Star and your intention, a script will be allowed to flow.

The Voyage West

Chapter 19

Anchor

Getting your bearings

The ship is released from its mooring. Take a moment with your notebook or ship's log to think about your voyage West and a study of story through the lens of Myth.

First of all, how are you doing right now as we begin? What is it like in your world today? What is nature up to? How is your tree? And how is the weather as we set sail on our metaphorical journey Westward-bound?

What does travelling West conjure up for you? How do you feel about going West? What does it mean to you to be heading off to this new place and to cross an ocean like this? We have time at sea until we find the West spot and take the *Story Compass* flag out onto the land.

When you think about archetypes what happens within you? Does anyone appear in your mind's eye? How do you feel about the idea of there being a realm where all the archetypes live together?

On this ship that is your body or context, you can relate to the archetype through a body that has been born from the Mythical and brought into this story of life. You are about to set sail with your ship of life with all that is in the storylines of Myth behind you: Just you and the stories of Myth together on board. It could get pretty busy on board this ship!

What do you see before you as the Mythical realm? Where does the place of Myth appear in relationship to you? When we talk about the Secret Archetype who is it that steps out of the shadows? What is the atmosphere like when the archetypes are given the space to be? When the Empowered Archetype is mentioned, who or what do you envision? Can you feel the potential of great findings from this study of story when we focus on the Mythical influence? I wonder what the study will bring to shore when we later disembark.

Ethos

Your task this week is to really ground in the Visionary *Story Compass* practice. The visionary way is to be in a space where we can both be present with what is and also be ready and equipped to be in touch with information and understanding that comes from the bigger picture.

In Anchor, you are invited to continue to set up space, practice being present with your tree and allow yourself to be in sync with the rhythm of nature as you acclimatize more to a way of working and holding yourself.

A simple formula

So again, we begin again with the practice of being present. Then the triangle of knowing, nature and trust are the principles that follow presence. With Myth, it is the centre of the triangle and the place of Presence that we encourage to come alive as the course develops as a character anchor to help the Story work to unfold.

Presence

Presence is the central pole of the entire visionary practice. It is what runs throughout everything. Presence is the act of being present, of not running away or rushing. It is the act of unconditionally and, whilst holding awareness and compassion, being able to be present with what is.

Over this time, practice noticing when you are present and when you are in a place different to presence. What does it take to move yourself back to presence again each time you notice you are not present? When do you find yourself most easily present? Make some notes.

Nature

Sit with your back to the special tree you have found, or visualise yourself there. Take some time to become present. Focus on your breath and simply become mindful to what chatter inside your head might be going on. Presence is about allowing awareness to arise and comes from a different place to the mind chatter.

Let yourself move into your senses. Touch - feel the air on your skin, touch the ground with your fingers and the surface of the tree, grass and nature around you. Smell - breath in the scents. Taste - taste the air, lick the grass, bark, a flower. Hearing - let your ears take in the sounds. Sight - let your eyes cast on everything as if seeing for the first time. Let nature join you through your senses.

In this space, bring yourself to become aware of being present and in the moment. You are looking to become present with nature both within and without. Now imagine this presence as being able to exist throughout all times. Take yourself to the beginnings of everything. Feel the origins. Feel the today. Allow a conversation to happen moving with presence with your senses and nature through these two stations of presence.

Bring yourself back. How do you feel about nature now?

Knowing

Pick up your drum or rattle. You can visualise a bubble of light around you that holds presence. Set the intention that you are only available here to connect with your knowing. Choose a colour to coat the bubble around you that sets the boundary that this is a clear space for you. You can extend a second bubble to go all around your home and the boundaries of the land around your home and set the same intention. Sit and connect with being present again. You will get to know what this feeling is like the more that you practice these concepts of being.

Now focus on your knowing. Think of a time when you have known something. You can begin to drum or rattle. (You will do this for about fifteen minutes) Connect with your knowing and let all your attention and the attention of the drum beat flow to hold awareness for this knowing. Ask yourself 'Where does this knowing come from? Feel the origins and authenticity of your knowing. Let it strengthen and take its place. Observe what happens for you.

You can also do this with by playing a drumming track if you don't have a drum.

Come back and thank your drum and the space that held you. Take some notes.

Trust

Return to your place in nature. Move into a place of presence again. Be in your senses. Take some time to land and be with the earth and the weather. Feel yourself as a part of this wider system. Now open up to feeling the interconnectedness of everything. Become aware of the different systems within the outer nature operating right now. Feel how they work together and the plan that they are a part of. Feel into your trust for this plan.

Now feel all of the systems going on within you and your body, mind, emotions, passions. Feel your organs and your blood flow, the beating of your heart, your lungs breathing, your eyes and the way your thoughts respond to your eyes working. Feel how you connect with the outer world through your lungs and your sight and thoughts, your sense of smell and your emotions.

Move back again to your awareness of the systems in nature outside of you and the plan everything including you is a part of. Feel into your trust for this plan. Spend about fifteen minutes in this being with trust. Come out of the task and then make some notes on how you found this and any insights you had.

Chapter 20

Sea

Mythical Life

Let's return to what you have found to bring the sea (your life) into your home. Remind yourself of the Pole Star intention you have for this *Story Compass* book. As we are working with story and opening awareness and understandings in the story of ourselves and the worlds we interact with it is important to take it slowly, make it creative and appealing. Something to remember is that with the focus on our own mythology comes the natural premise that we each have the right to take ownership and responsibility for our individual myth and life force. You are in charge of your choices - no one else! This means you can decide what you are in a place to do. You can choose whether to bring your life's material to the play and the project or whether to step back and simply be present in the now (e.g., sit and anchor with our tree and nature).

In the sea work we set up our space again as playwrights! You will need your notebook and your box that you have your dressing room inside and the intention to keep on making and collecting props and costumes. At sea, this is where your story wardrobe and stage set design continues to build.

Resourcing

Once again, we begin by building resources. Healing work can happen because a safe, accepting space is set up. Things can only safely come out into the light because the space we create is caring and strong whilst providing all the resources that are needed.

This time, complete the tasks yourself and then ask someone else to try this task with you too. Take some notes on what you discover working with another person.

What follows, is the first task that the Good Ship Story recommends in the Sea section.

1. Life boats

Connect with presence. If presence were to be a character, what character would they be? What would presence wear, feel like, sound like or smell like? What would they be called? Make some notes!

As you open up to presence, ask presence to really tune in and make a list. Make a list of things that help you to be in tune with being present. Ask your sense of presence to add some extras that you know will be good for you to have in there too.

Here are some examples:

- Feel my bare feet on the earth
- Take deep breaths connecting with the air
- Watch clouds
- Touch the material of my clothes and the surfaces of everything I come into contact with
- Let my eyes really take in the details of the world around me
- Smell flowers
- Pick pebbles up and hold them
- Mop the floor
- Set up a still life and draw it
- Make a cartoon strip of my day
- Swim in the sea
- Play a musical instrument
- Drum
- Eat outdoors

Have a go at your own. Make it your presence lifeboat list for when the sea gets choppy and the going gets overwhelming.

Make it your go-to. Put down all thoughts of looking for meaning or 'doing the book' when you get to these places.

How do you feel having this list here now? What does it tell you about what is important and nourishing for you in your connection to presence in your life? How much do you allow yourself to be present and apply this way of listening to your needs generally? What do you realise about your archetypal expression and your connection to presence in your life lived from this task? Are you able to connect and feel the pulse of the Mythical coming through yet?

2. Life View

In West, the simple exercise and method introduced to bring your life into view is a study of the plays and theatres of your life.

Take two big sheets of paper and write down the title on one 'Plays I am a part of' and on the other one 'Theatres I perform in'. Have a think about what these titles mean for you and where this exercise may be going for a while. Now think about your Empowered Author that you have located in your work with North. Ask your Empowered Author to be an overseer and a protector for you with this piece of work.

Take a rattle that you can rattle as you tune in to this exercise. Or, you might choose to play a drumming track instead. I recommend you spend ten to fifteen minutes in the following task.

Feel a protective pale blue orb all around you before you start this piece of tuning in. Set the intention that you are held in a soothing, loving and watery light that can cleanse and keep you connected to love as you work through this. If at any time the exercise becomes too intense, then simply feel yourself going back to that pale blue light and come out of the exercise. You can go back in when you feel calm or ready.

Please also set the intention that you are only available to connect to what you feel ready to open to. Know that you are the one in charge here and if you feel yourself go somewhere that is overwhelming, then let your Empowered Author know you need them to stand between you and what you are encountering and gently bring yourself out of the task to bathe in the pale blue.

Imagine your special tree behind you, grounding you and holding a space to take away anything that you can now release and bring in extra earth energy as is needed. You could also choose to do this outside with your tree, wearing earphones.

As the drumming plays, or as you rattle, open up to connect with the earth beneath you, your tree and feel yourself grounded and held. Then open to be aware of your own body's energetic field. Feel the physical, emotional, mental, passionate and different spiritual expressions of you as a field. You might also include your chakras in this with your base chakra the physical, your sacral chakra the emotional, solar plexus the passionate, heart chakra the mental and then your throat, third eye and crown the ethereal, astral and stellar spiritual expressions. Let your self take time to connect with each of these. After two or three minutes, you will possibly feel like your aura is a glowing field of radiating energy. Feel the power of this.

You are now going to imagine all of the different plays and theatres of your life that you are a part of and that you perform within. The plays can be things like 'the family play'; 'the mother daughter play'; 'the school friendship play'; 'the university play'; 'the good girl play' etc. The theatres could be things like school, city, nature, education systems, family life, home, spiritual domain etc. Try not to have preconceived ideas and see what naturally shows itself. Also, be gentle with yourself and know that this work can be tender. If you feel it is overwhelming, then ask your guide of unconditional love to shine light into places, feel the Empowered Author standing between you and what you feel the overwhelm with and feel the tree balancing and grounding you. You can also choose to do this activity step by step, if it feels like that would be easier for you.

You are now going to imagine all of the plays and theatres of your life lived so far. Tune into the idea that you in this place right now in your current story is driven by all of the plays and theatres you have ever been in. Feel your life around you as the circle of your life lived from conception until the present moment. Take some minutes to honour this. This is your creation and your experience. How cool and amazing is that?

Take some time to let your lifeline land. Then in your own time, ask to become aware of some of the plays and theatres that you have been a part of in your life. Keep open to seeing what is there.

Know that the job is to simply see them there and honour their presence. You can bow to them to convey that you mean them no harm.

After you feel complete, then bow to everything and let your Empowered Author know that you are ready to disconnect now. Allow the plays and theatres to dissolve. Move back to feeling your own space of being shining brightly and then move back into feeling at home in your physical body. Thank your tree and everything that is holding space for you.

Reach over to the papers you have set aside with the title 'Plays I am a part of' and 'Theatres I perform in'. Make a shape for 'you' in the centre of the paper. Be immediate with your charting now! Try not to think too much about it, but with different colours of pencils or pens, begin to draw some shapes for the different plays you have met in the exercise. Label them so you can remember what they refer to. Take your time but work intuitively and without questioning yourself. Now do the same for theatres.

On completion of this task, take some time to study what you have drawn. Notice how the plays or theatres overlap and how big or small they each are. Think about the significance of the colours you have chosen for each or patterns you have drawn within them. Notice how close or far away you place each of them in relation to you.

Are you surprised by what has come up here? Does marking them down in this way help you to have increased awareness about the archetypal way you have been living your life at all? How do you feel now? Make some notes.

Sit in the silence for a while. Thank the Pole Star, your true nature and your lifeline for all that they hold.

Creative Theatre

If you were to design a programme for each of these plays what would they look like? What images would they have on them? What colours and what fonts would they be in? What would the architecture for each theatre be like? How many would the theatres seat? Would they be indoor or outdoor? See if you can create some sketches.

Over these weeks, bring through some programme and theatre building simple ideas that you can introduce to your stage and props department that you can work with to allow yourself and others to explore the notion of archetypal playing with theatres and plays of life as a concept.

What have you learnt about story and what is coming up as archetypal themes from this exercise?

Chapter 21

Ship

It is time to meet our guest for Direction West.

As we put our focus on to ship, the physical carrier, the body and the liver of your life, we open our work to meet and learn from a new archetype who becomes the ship's context for us all.

Our guest this time is Anansi, the original maker of stories of the Ashanti people in Ghana. The stories of Anansi were later passionately told though the Afro-Caribbean communities where Anansi represented an empowering force towards the abolition of slavery. Anansi is the Akan name for spider. He is originally a trickster God and is considered to be the 'Keeper of all Knowledge of Stories'.

I personally know Anansi through my work teaching in Inner City Birmingham in the early 1990s. I taught for a while in a wonderful school in Handsworth Wood, with a community where many of the families were African Caribbean and West African in origin. I taught all subjects, but was the Art person in the school and one of my tasks was to write proposals to get funding for Art projects. I created a project working with Anansi stories. An Artist was commissioned to come in and replicate children's designs to make a mural in the school. We immersed ourselves in the tales of Anansi and the children wrote their own Anansi stories. For a while all of our lessons had Anansi themes. Anansi became our teacher for a while! Whilst I can't claim to be as connected to the source of these stories as many of the members of my classroom, I was deeply inspired by Anansi and the spirit of revolution, impenetrable power and intelligence that I sensed from the storytellers of those who worked with Anansi medicine. It is only now, writing this book that I am beginning to look back and reflect on what Anansi freed in me.

I actually went to West Africa around the time of the project and encountered the trickster energy within and outside of my self.

So, back to narrator now!

Here we have him, the Spider of ultimate freedom and intelligence; the one who understands the zany and illogical, healing ways of the West. I officially welcome my old friend Anansi. I don't have the spiel that Anansi has, Anansi's spirit is filtered through my English lingo. Perhaps one day someone will help me with the poetics and nuance of an Afro-Caribbean lilt. But my heart is with Anansi and I hope I can do him the respectful justice he deserves.

There is such a feeling of joy and anticipation on this ship right now as we feel Anansi's approach! The air is opening and it is like more sunshine is coming through. Can you hear the steel pans? Are you noticing how the colours are becoming more vibrant?

Oh wow! Look right up high! There is an opening in the sky. From it there is a long silver thread with a dot at the end of it. The dot comes closer and becomes bigger and bigger and bigger, until we see a black hairy mass with a mischievous grin, bright eyes and eight hairy legs bestowed with big black shiny boots. With a scuffle and a prance Anansi lands, his legs breaking into a tap dance that beats a rhythm through the deck. The drums become quiet. We remark at the startling music the tap dance brings and notice that we are moving into a bit of a trance. The drum is in his foot movements. Anansi stops, bows and takes off his hat. He stands before us, continuing to grin.

Anansi

Anansi speaks.

"Nice to meet ya! It's so great to be here on this boat with you travelling West. I heard the call to open up the Mythical realm with

you all and I just had to be here as the speaker for this brilliant vat of wonder that is Storyland.

You know, once there was no stories at all in the world. Can you imagine that? No story? It was pretty boring; I have to tell you. Boring not just by my standards! You can understand that with me and my loving for fun and mischief, it really had to be me that got the stories back! I'll tell you the story about that.

It was that greedy Sky-God, Nyame - he had them all!

I decided to pay him a visit.

So, I, Anansi goes to Nyame and asks how much the stories would cost to buy. Oh, my lord, Nyame set a high price! I only had to bring to him Onini the Python, Osebo the Leopard, the Mmoboro Hornets, and Mmoatia the dwarf. Poof! What a job I had on my hands.

But I am not one to ever be defeated. So, what else could I do? I be bound to set about capturing these essential beings to claim my prize of freeing the stories from the Sky God.

First, I went to where Python lived. I stood outside his tree and debated out loud whether Python was really longer than the palm branch or not (as his wife, Aso, says). So, Python overheard and, when I carefully explained to Python about the debate, well, he agreed to lie along the palm branch. Beautiful! Because Python cannot easily make himself completely straight, you can imagine that a true impression of his actual length is difficult to obtain, so then I got Python to agree to be tied to the branch. I tied him to it so carefully and nicely. And so there I had him, ha! I carts him back to Nyame as he is hissing away.

Well, it was leopard next. To catch leopard, I dug a deep hole in the ground. Leopard fell in the hole of course and there was I, at the rescue 'Let me help you out', I said 'I can use my webs'. So, leopard came out of that one nicely bound up and I carries him away too.

To catch the hornets, well, I just filled a calabash with water and poured some over a banana leaf I held over my head and then some over the nest. 'It be raining!' I calls. The hornets were scared, they didn't want to lose their nest to a flood. 'Why don't you,' I very helpfully enquired of the hornets, 'get into the empty calabash?' Well, they obliged and I just quickly sealed the opening.

To catch the dwarf, I had the idea to create a doll and to cover it with sticky gum. I places the doll under the odum tree where the dwarves play and put some yam in a bowl in front of it. Along comes the dwarf. She ate the yam and thanked the doll, which of course did not reply. Hahaha she was so annoyed at its bad manners! She struck it, ouch, first with one hand then the other. The hands stuck and hey presto that was her captured also.

So, I hands my captives over to Nyame. Then I got the stories given to me in a pot. Yay!

So, I goes back home with all the stories in the world stored in this huge pot. It was quite a struggle to carry the pot, you can imagine. Nyame, despite his own selfish nature had given me the instruction to share the stories with everyone. Can you believe that? Mental.

Well, I thought I would just have a look for myself first. Every day, I looked in the pot. Every day, I learned different things. The pot was full of wonderful ideas and skills. I felt so entertained and happy.

So, I liked this so much, I decides not to share the treasure of knowledge with everyone but to keep all the wisdom for myself!

My new plan was to hide the wisdom on top of a tall tree. First, I took some vines and made some strong string and tied it firmly *around the pot, leaving one end free. Then I tied the loose end around my waist so that the pot hung in front of me. Then I starts to climb the tree. It was a bit of a struggle again because the pot of wisdom keeps getting in my way, bumping against my tummy.*

I have seven sons, you know? Well, one of them, he was watching in fascination as he saw me, his father trying to get up the tree. And my son, he told me "If you tie the pot to your back, it will be easier to cling to the tree and climb."

So, that's what I did. I continued to climb the tree, with much more ease than before.

But then I got to the top of the tree, and I was really angry. 'A young one with some common sense knows more than I, and I have the pot of wisdom!" Poof. What a load of rubbish. There was no wisdom in this pot!

I throws down the pot of wisdom! Stupid pot! The pot breaks, and pieces of wisdom fly in every direction. People came and they find the bits scattered everywhere. They scoops it up and they also take some home to their families and friends.

So, they say, this is why to this day, no one person has all the world's wisdom. People everywhere share small pieces of it whenever they exchange ideas.

Hmm, I am always freeing. I can't help myself. Maybe, I keeps the stories but they live through you.

Thank you for hearing my story. Take some time to let it land.

Get yourself a drum now or put on some West-African drumming or steel pan music. Let the story I have just told sink in. Come on, stand by me and feel me and my spider senses here right in front of you. Feel yourself connect to the impressive web of all of the archetypal possibilities and storylines that could ever be. Wow at the presence of that which has awakened in you from the listening to what I have shared with you just now. Ask this presence to spin a protective cocoon all about your body and energetic field. This cocoon will set a signal for safety. It will permit you only to connect with what is healing and good.

Ask yourself - what was the part that you got in the shattering of that pot?

Now feel me here as you drum or fall into the music and attune to the wisdom that came to you when the stories came through to the world. I am going to let go of my impression now. I am clear Anansi energy with no form or name. As you permit this energy to open without a form, remember I am an expression of intelligence and the playfulness of a deeper way. Ask this intelligence and playfulness to merge with you. Permit this energy to awaken the wisdom storyteller within you and the true intelligence and inclination to play that is your own. Feel how I stimulate and awaken the power of the one who is connected to finding a way through mischief and play. Feel your dignity man! Let me be with you for ten minutes now of your time, drinking my energy deep and allowing it to illuminate the origins of the strong blazing wisdom blaster that you are. Only after that time will you let me go, thank me but let the experience of what has been lightened inside you remain and be strong."

Anansi stands back and observes and supports as the energy you awaken to be with inspired by Anansi and this story allows an opening. After this piece of work is complete, he goes to rest in a shady corner and tap dances again.

Narrator

I invite you to make some notes. What did your merging with the one whose intelligence and playfulness works in a powerful and Mythical way allow in you? What is happening for you now? How has the experience of embodying mischief and wisdom changed your perspective on archetypal forces and the exercise with plays and theatres? Have any of these plays or theatres lost their hold? How has this experience of embodying contributed to your understanding of story?

Has the support of this story and the Archetype of this

realm - Anansi - and the focus on a higher intelligence and play, allowed an appreciation of how you have been relating with the Mythical?

For the rest of this week and in certain situations, choose to reconnect with clear energy of Anansi and merge with this again. Notice and take notes on how this affects you and the plays that have captured you. Remember how nothing is too much for Anansi and how his creativity and defiance is legendary. Remember how nothing beats him. Are there any aspects of you that you are sensing strengthening and standing no nonsense?

Chapter 22

Map

Let's take your life for a swim in the sea of life that surrounds our ship. Soon, you will be going into the Mythical in nature and your dreams to begin to map the worlds.

Mapping will become an aid for allowing what is important and true to the way you live to come to the surface. There are three methods you will employ for investigative Story work: vision tracking, mapping and movement.

1. Vision Tracking

Nature is a great keeper of the Mythical! When we connect with nature as a living being alongside ourselves, we can more easily access ourselves as a part of a Mythical landscape.

In Vision Tracking, you are invited to find a staff from a tree of your own choosing, put on a hat and set out Story walking. Vision Tracking is a practice of moving out into the landscape with a question and then seeing where the vision of the question leads you and making notes. The result is a prescription from nature for whatever you are feeling or asking for a solution for.

You can do this exercise as a walk in the hills, through your local neighbourhood or even on a bus. Ask the question and then just see what turns up for you. Make notes and then collect your information on what you find to make a little story prescription from on your return.

You might find acorns, see a squirrel, smell a bonfire, pass someone and overhear the saying 'My mum cooks lovely lasagne' and lots more. Your story might begin something like 'The squirrel's mother had made a lovely lasagne for dinner, but Squirrel was out looking for acorns and was needing to build a fire. Something was ready to be burned away…'

Look for the message in what you intuitively put together on your return.

2. Mapping

We are going to map our dreams. You have already created lots of maps in the Sea section. So, you have a lot of resources for Mapping work already. Dreams are the place where we truly enter the Mythical through other doors, so it is a great place to go to for information and story changing work.

If you don't remember dreams, then just set the tasks for yourself anyway and trust that your unconscious will be working out everything in the other worlds. In this case, be alert to how you might feel different in your everyday life as a result of the mapping dreams exercise.

When you go to sleep on a night, set the intention to connect to the rivers, seas and/or the water channels or lakes in your local environment. You can also sleep with a hazel branch by your bed to help with this divining. Ask the waters to help you to open up to your Mythical landscape and to help you to become more and more in harmony with your Mythical nature. You might also as in the exercise above, take a question or a healing intention into this task.

Keep a notepad and pen by your bed. As soon as you wake up record everything you can remember about your dreams for 4 mornings. If you don't remember anything, then produce a random drawing or a string of words that come out.

After four days, make a visual map of the material in the dreams or the post-dreaming download onto paper. What do you find out from this exercise?

Sometimes it can take steady intention with dreams for a flow to happen. You may wish to continue this task for a number of weeks and see what is produced over a longer time span.

3. Movement

So now you can use both of the above exercises material to work with movement; Nature movement. Your task with nature and movement is to become as one with one of the prescriptive elements from your nature vision-tracking task. Bring it into movement with music. Let something flow.

Get a long sheet or light muslin scarf. The cloth or scarf is going to be the dream. Again, if you have no information from your dream, go with what flowed when you first woke up.

Ask the cloth or scarf to show you what the dream was pulling through from the Mythical realm. By allowing the cloth to be the dream for you, you can build a relationship with the Mythical domain. Feeling the realms communicating. Be aware of how the cloth brings you closer and closer to the dream world and the Mythical realm until eventually you feel yourself able to be the cloth and the dream world of Myth. Hopefully you will find yourself realising that the two are not as separate as we are conditioned to believe them to be!

How do you feel now after the movement tasks?

Chapter 23

Story Study

In Story Study the task of allowing discernment with story becomes the focus. The Story Practice is with the Secret Archetype and the Empowered Archetype.

The Secret archetype is a power that you are not aware of who is unconsciously hidden in your life and drives scripts.

The Empowered archetype is a power that is strong in you. They are synonymous with the metaphorical and the Mythical. Connecting with them can bring magic and alchemy to your life.

Anansi leads this exercise.

Stepping out of the Shadows

"So, let's see you truly! Come across to this shady corner where spiders like to weave their webs. I have some gossamer circles for you, woven from the finest spider web threads. I am placing them so that you can stand on them like islands.

Let's open the Story Wheel again. Pick up your rattle and whistle. Off you go. Remember the spiel?

I rattle and whistle. I face and call the North and the Place of the Author and the Keepers of the North, place of the present and the physical realm. You are all so welcome. Thank you for being here.

I rattle and whistle. I face and call the East and the Place of the Life stories and the Keepers of the East, place of the lifeline. You are all so welcome. Thank you for being here.

I rattle and whistle. I face and call the South and the Place of the Ancestral stories and the Keepers of the South the ancestral banks. You are all so welcome. Thank you for being here.

I rattle and whistle. I face and call the West and the Place of Myth and the Keepers of the West the Pillars of light as archetypal forces. You are all so welcome. Thank you for being here.

I call the Centre and know that this is also the circle. A circle of light surrounds this space. An orb of light surrounds this space. This space is a place of wholeness. This is a space beyond all stories and contains all that goes beyond what we can ever possibly know.

This space is clear. It brings deep listening. All that is pure and true holds it. This space is open.

Take some time to become present now. Feel a grove of trees all around this space. Feel the knowing inside you listening and holding space with you. Stand on one of the gossamer circles. Focus on presence and Power. And as you do so, take time to see what comes to surface as the story you bring that is stopping you from sinking into relationship with the present moment and the power of you. Let your feelings and thoughts take you to where you need to go in this sacred Story Wheel. Feel the orb of wholeness and the grove of trees holding you safely.

Become aware of the gossamer circles in this environment of the Secret Archetype, the Empowered Archetype and I, Anansi. Take some notes on how you feel right now and what is coming up for you. Keep your connection with presence and your own power as you move through the following.

Now what you are going to do is to move to stand on each of the gossamer circles in turn and just ask that they bring their information and medicine to whatever you have brought to this meeting with your focus on presence. Spend two or three minutes or more in the story field of each circle.

Begin with the Secret Archetype. Who is there that you never knew before? Take your time. Take two or three minutes to tune in.

Take your position on the circle of the Empowered Archetype. What does the Empowered Archetype bring for you and your power?

Now to my circle! Mine is the circle of the one who knows the way of trickery and illusion and who takes no messing! What comes as medicine for you and your power here? This can be your opportunity to bring healing to something in your story and to free the space to hold dignity and strength.

When you feel you have a sense of what you have been able to access, go back to the circle that is for you. Write a story about power or permit a free flowing story happen. I will wait right here until you have come to the end of writing your story.

So, you have finished? Brilliant! Thanks to everything for holding this space. The space and the Story Wheel session is now closed."

And with this, Anansi scuffles along tapping his boots on the deck and picks up the circles. Then, he shoots upwards and launches a thread of gossamer up into the sky. It clings to an invisible force and he is pulled vertically up and far, far away to be a distant speck again. Then he vanishes from sight.

Narrator

Thank you, Anansi. Thank you for freeing and sharing the stories, for your mischievous and crafty ways and for your eternal dignity. Thank you for helping us to live our archetypal power and to understand even better the Craft of Story.

See if you can make some more notes. What did this exercise show you about archetypes and the influence of the secret and empowered archetypes? What do you need to do now to complete? Is there anything you need to do to make some changes in your life or to help you to remember something important to carry forwards?

Chapter 24

Excavation and Findings

We have travelled as far West as we can! We find ourselves in the middle of water. But it is time to disembark. Ah don't worry! Here is some scuba diving gear and a special guide, Seal, who has popped up to greet us. Get the gear on. It's ok. You will find when you jump in you will find the equipment is super advanced and there is oxygen in the tank to last for days. This is Mythical territory of course!

Come on, get the flag that says Myth. Don't worry it will dissolve into the Mythical again as soon as we leave. Stick it in those clips on the left of the tank on your back. Perfect! Right, get those flippers walking across the deck. Narrator does the oxygen and fitting checks. Yep. It is all perfect. Breathe the oxygen now. Wonderful. There's a little slide appeared look. You can slip yourself off the side of the ship and down a slipway that's not too steep. Seal is waiting for you. Wheee! And we are in!

Seal wants us to go downwards. The sun is shining through the water and it is so beautiful in here. You can see the different bright coloured fish swimming about. There is a torch on your headgear and it shines brightly to the depths below. You follow Seal and Seal takes you into a beautiful underwater cavern.

There are lights shining in the cavern. The ground is cushioned by vibrant green and soft, mossy seaweed. You see two throne seats with two tridents by them. It is the throne seats of the Goddess and the God of the Sea! Seal gestures for you to sit in one of them and to hold one of the tridents in your hands. Music begins to come through earphones that are a part of the headpiece you are wearing. You feel yourself going into trance and the trident in your hands with its three points becoming antennae for special information about the Mythical lands. You find yourself downloading an attunement from the Goddess or God of the sea that seals your connection to your true archetypal nature.

Stay here for ten to fifteen minutes and feel the power of this download. Ask for guidance and even more understanding about story and the work you can do on the Good Ship Story and beyond. Give these throne seats in the Western Cavern your intention you held for working with this book. Ask to be brought even more enlightenment.

At the end of your journey, you feel Seal nudge you. You let go of the trident and its special powers and leave a note of thanks for the Goddess and God of the sea to receive on their return. Back up you go in the direction of the light that comes from the sun shining form the heights of the sky above. You return to the deck. You take a shower and then redress to sail back home. You take notes.

Getting ready for the completion

Find yourself for the last time, at the ship's wheel. Imagine your tree behind your back. Feel present. Acknowledge presence as a character and everything that you have found out about that are Myth's part to play in Story work.

Moving out of the harbour and this estuary here takes a while, but eventually you find yourself in a place where there is just sea again all about you.

Soon it will be time to head right back to where you began. First of all, take some time with the Mythical, your understanding of archetypes now and the ship's log. Feel your Myth as the eternal story that it is. How brilliant that you can take the learning from Author, Lifeline, Ancestors and Myth and have almost completed the circle. Have a look at what you have learnt in the land of Myth. Maybe you can create doodles, drawings or put together some more collages in your notebook. Ask the archetypes what has become. Report it all back in your ship's log.

Soon you will be homeward bound.

Chapter 25

Sailing Safely Home

So here we are at last ready to return. What a journey we have made! You begin to sail. Here on the ocean, the homeland is in sight. You set course towards it. As we head across, here are some reflections on some of the things to think about and some reminders of the journey pointers, before you step on land again as someone who understands more deeply the Way of Story.

One of the things I have found through my years as a Teacher, Counsellor, Constellation Practitioner and Visionary Worker, is that if you are going to walk into territory that involves change, then you need a good strong theatre, a clear structure, a faith in the container and the availability to be present for someone exactly as they are.

Here in *Story Compass*, the theatre has been the ship's deck and the journey to the 4Directions. The clear structure has been the working through the tasks of the six weeks. The container is the 4Directions Story Wheel and the simple availability to 'be present and with' has been the ethos of the book all the way through. You are the Author and you are ultimately in charge!

Here are some steps and questions you might ask yourself every time you set up space for yourself or for someone else.

1. Theatre

What is the theatre? How can you set up your space to be interesting and available for the person you work with? I remember going to the house of Sigmund Freud, allegedly the father of psychotherapy, in Swiss Cottage, London and loving seeing his room set up with archetypal figures, rich cultural patterns and lots of natural materials. It inspired me to fill my workspace with more of these visual cues for imagination and opening to Mythological associations. Try designing a workspace, or if you work online, a background you can create, that works with the idea of a theatre that supports the Story work you do.

2. Clear Structure

Here is a reminder of the clear structure I provided you with in this work. I recommend you work with it and weave it with your own. Most important is the lifeboats section. We all need to feel safe to go into these areas and knowing that we have some grounding things to do to come back into our lives in a way that feels pleasurable can make us more willing to open in new ways.

North Star

Setting of an intention for the journey ahead.

Anchor

Visionary ethos triangle model: nature, knowing and trust with presence.

Sea

Lifeboat list making.
    Map-making to find ways to bring your life into view.

Ship

Some work with a major archetype. Drumming or playing music and simple movement to embody the archetype and become aware of how you stand in the everyday world.

Map

Mapping becomes an aid for allowing what is there to come to the surface. Some ways:

- Writing
- Miming
- Speaking
- Acting
- Drawing
- Mapping
- Multi-sensory
- Movement
- Taking a walk
- Nature responding
- Vision tracking
- Listening and responding

Story Study

Story Study is with the Secret and Empowered aspects of whatever you are working with.

Work with chairs, mats and costume to allow a simple disentangling practice. You might also choose to draw or paint this process too.

Excavation and Findings

Provide an invitation to complete and reflect back on the story journey with the North Star as the guide. Look at what has become clearer and learnt that can be supportive.

3. Container

Here is the reminder of the exercise for opening the 4Directions Story Wheel. This helps to create a space of wholeness and safety to work inside.

I rattle and whistle. I face and call the North and the Place of the Author and the Keepers of the North, place of the present and the physical realm. You are all so welcome. Thank you for being here.

I rattle and whistle. I face and call the East and the Place of the Life stories and the Keepers of the East, place of the lifeline. You are all so welcome. Thank you for being here.

I rattle and whistle. I face and call the South and the Place of the Ancestral stories and the Keepers of the South the ancestral banks. You are all so welcome. Thank you for being here.

I rattle and whistle. I face and call the West and the Place of Myth and the Keepers of the West the Pillars of light as archetypal forces. You are all so welcome. Thank you for being here.

I call the Centre and know that this is also the circle. A circle of light surrounds this space. An orb of light surrounds this space. This space is a place of wholeness. This is a space beyond all stories and contains all that goes beyond what we can ever possibly know.

This space is clear. It brings deep listening. All that is pure and true holds it. This space is open.

Take some time to become present now. Feel a grove of trees all around this space. Feel the knowing inside you listening and holding space with you.

Remember at the end of each session to close the space again and thank everything for showing up. I usually ask that everything can feel the benefit of this work through all the realms.

4. Availability to be Present

Here, you have to scoop up all of your many roles and choose presence for yourself or with the person you are working with first and foremost. Holding curiosity and acceptance is a good tip here. From this and with all that is set out above, then the journey can just unfold. Here is a reminder of the roles you will be shifting between throughout.

The Artist is encouraged to create and respond. The Story Weaver is encouraged to listen and to open expressive flow. The Visionary Operator opens up the medicine wheel and invites in the perspectives of the different realms. The Counsellor holds presence and unconditional appreciation and wonder. The Constellation Practitioner learns the ways of disentanglement and the power of giving names and places to things to bring freedom and autonomy.

A Simple Practice

Finally, here is a reminder of the simple practice! All you need to do is set up the space, be aware of the roles and then know that what you are doing is simply raising awareness and allowing movements so that each person we work with can come into more of their true place.

Farewell

Thank you for sailing with me on this Ship of Great Adventure. Thank you for all you have opened to and shared with us all. Here we are approaching the dock now! Who has come to greet you? Screw up your eyes to see. Can you see their form? What are they wearing? Do you recognise them? Oh wow - what a gift! I don't seem to recognise anyone here and I know why! This must be your very own Story Archetype who has come to start you off on your own journey now as you step off the Good Ship Story!

Quick, throw them the rope so they can tie this ship to the shore. After taking one good long last glance around the deck where you have spent your time, you find yourself climbing off the ship. You step onto the homeland to walk with your very own Story Archetype as they guide you to a place on the shore that they know well. You will have so much to talk about and plan together.

When you look back, the ship is sailing merrily away into the distance again. It must be off to find its next adventurer. You hear a toot from its direction and you could swear you can see someone waving from the deck. Cheerio. Perhaps you will come back one day. Or perhaps you will set new ships to sail with your own Story Sailors. I hope so!

About the Author

Carol Day is an International Visionary Teacher, Artist and Author. She lives in Scotland, UK, where she directs the Centre for Creative Vision and 'Bringing in the Mythical' – an innovative Arts project. She is the creator of several nature-led models, bringing great effectiveness for students, clients, organisations and readers. With an MFA in Fine Art in Context and an MSc in Counselling, Carol contributes to contemporary research. As Psychotherapist, Constellation Facilitator and Shamanic Operator, she runs a successful private practice in Systemic Story Therapy. In 2000, she was one of Scotland's chosen artists for The Year of the Artist. In 2007 she co-designed the Nature as Teacher model for Scotland's first outdoor nursery which has won several awards. She has featured on Radio 4, Blues and Roots Radio and the British Autoethnography conference. Commissioned to generate ground breaking visionary Story programmes working with inclusive community ethos and land, she was the presenter of the 2020 film 'Story of Tatha'.

**MOON
BOOKS**

PAGANISM & SHAMANISM

What is Paganism? A religion, a spirituality, an alternative belief
system, nature worship? You can find support for all these defini-
tions (and many more) in dictionaries, encyclopaedias, and text
books of religion, but subscribe to any one and the truth will evade
you. Above all Paganism is a creative pursuit, an encounter with
reality, an exploration of meaning and an expression of the soul.
Druids, Heathens, Wiccans and others, all contribute their insights
and literary riches to the Pagan tradition. Moon Books invites you
to begin or to deepen your own encounter, right here, right now.
If you have enjoyed this book, why not tell other readers by
posting a review on your preferred book site.

Recent bestsellers from Moon Books are:

Journey to the Dark Goddess
How to Return to Your Soul
Jane Meredith
Discover the powerful secrets of the Dark Goddess and
transform your depression, grief and pain into healing
and integration.
Paperback: 978-1-84694-677-6 ebook: 978-1-78099-223-5

Shamanic Reiki
Expanded Ways of Working with Universal Life Force Energy
Llyn Roberts, Robert Levy
Shamanism and Reiki are each powerful ways of healing; together,
their power multiplies. *Shamanic Reiki* introduces techniques to
help healers and Reiki practitioners tap ancient healing wisdom.
Paperback: 978-1-84694-037-8 ebook: 978-1-84694-650-9

Pagan Portals – The Awen Alone
Walking the Path of the Solitary Druid
Joanna van der Hoeven
An introductory guide for the solitary Druid, *The Awen Alone* will
accompany you as you explore, and seek out your own place
within the natural world.
Paperback: 978-1-78279-547-6 ebook: 978-1-78279-546-9

A Kitchen Witch's World of Magical Herbs & Plants
Rachel Patterson
A journey into the magical world of herbs and plants, filled with
magical uses, folklore, history and practical magic. By popular
writer, blogger and kitchen witch, Tansy Firedragon.
Paperback: 978-1-78279-621-3 ebook: 978-1-78279-620-6

Medicine for the Soul
The Complete Book of Shamanic Healing
Ross Heaven
All you will ever need to know about shamanic healing and how to
become your own shaman...
Paperback: 978-1-78099-419-2 ebook: 978-1-78099-420-8

Shaman Pathways – The Druid Shaman
Exploring the Celtic Otherworld
Danu Forest
A practical guide to Celtic shamanism with exercises and
techniques as well as traditional lore for exploring the Celtic
Otherworld.
Paperback: 978-1-78099-615-8 ebook: 978-1-78099-616-5

Traditional Witchcraft for the Woods and Forests
A Witch's Guide to the Woodland with Guided Meditations and
Pathworking
Mélusine Draco
A Witch's guide to walking alone in the woods, with guided
meditations and pathworking.
Paperback: 978-1-84694-803-9 ebook: 978-1-84694-804-6

Naming the Goddess
Trevor Greenfield
Naming the Goddess is written by over eighty adherents and
scholars of Goddess and Goddess Spirituality.
Paperback: 978-1-78279-476-9 ebook: 978-1-78279-475-2

Shapeshifting into Higher Consciousness
Heal and Transform Yourself and Our World with Ancient
Shamanic and Modern Methods
Llyn Roberts
Ancient and modern methods that you can use every day to
transform yourself and make a positive difference in the world.
Paperback: 978-1-84694-843-5 ebook: 978-1-84694-844-2

Readers of ebooks can buy or view any of these bestsellers by
clicking on the live link in the title. Most titles are published in
paperback and as an ebook. Paperbacks are available in traditional
bookshops. Both print and ebook formats are available online.

Find more titles and sign up to our readers' newsletter at
http://www.johnhuntpublishing.com/paganism
Follow us on Facebook at https://www.facebook.com/MoonBooks
and Twitter at https://twitter.com/MoonBooksJHP